ADVANCE PRAISE

"Gen Z is about to take the workplace with new ideas, new ways of working and developing, including how they lead. This book provides the recipe for success in the new workplace and shares essential knowledge for the integration of emotional development and human behavior. A must read."

–Keith Ferrazzi
#1 *New York Times* best-selling author of *Competing in the New World of Work*, Executive and Team Coach, Speaker

"Wagner's book democratizes leadership in the workplace in support of a new generation of leaders who are teaming up in the co-creation of the future of work. In today's world of work everyone is a leader and this book equips organizations to leverage this huge potential. Wagner promotes a dynamic talent strategy that will lead to better business results."

–Dave Stafford
Former CHRO & CTO, Michelin North America

"This book activates leadership at all levels of the organization and promotes the co-creation of a new mindset. Wagner rightly advocates for the transformation of the workforce by creating the conditions for high performing cultures to emerge. A valuable integration of emotional development and human behavior in the workplace."

–Hitendra Wadhwa, PhD
Best-selling author of *Inner Mastery, Outer Success*, professor at Columbia Business School and founder of Mentora Institute.

"Wagner describes the future-ready organization and declares that everyone is a leader in the formation of a blended workforce that's tightly aligned to collective success. In the new workplace, all professionals co-create value, share expertise, and empower each other beyond organizational boundaries. This is a book for inclusive leaders of the cross-generational workforce."

–Frank Congiu
Senior Executive, Global Clients, Randstad USA

"*Leading to Succeed* is an insightful exploration into the essence of personal and professional growth. As an expert in group dynamics, I find this book to be a powerful tool in understanding the interplay between social-emotional intelligence, systems thinking, and leadership. It offers a unique perspective on shaping a meaningful career path by aligning one's inner values and worldview with outward actions. This comprehensive guide is pivotal for anyone aiming to navigate the evolving landscapes of modern workplaces with authenticity and purpose."

>   –**Tyrome Smith, MA**
>   Eco-Leadership Executive Coach, AK Rice Institute Group Relations Consultant

"Wagner Denuzzo is one of the top leading voices in career development, workforce planning, organizational growth and future of work. In *Leading to Succeed* Wagner distills his experience and career into an insightful guide that transcends the conventional boundaries of career advice for the future of work. His deep understanding of the evolving workplace, the new demands of work and jobs, the future of work, and the human element, shines through each page, making this book not just a read but an enlightening experience. Whether it's individual growth or organizational dynamics, Wagner's approach is both practical and profound, offering readers a unique perspective on how to navigate and excel in today's ever-changing professional landscape by investing in the skills needed for the future. This book is a testament to his dedication and skill in empowering people and organizations to realize their fullest potential."

>   —**Enrique Rubio**
>   Founder, Hacking HR

LEADING
TO
SUCCEED

Essential Skills for the New Workplace

WAGNER DENUZZO

credentia
press

Hardcover ISBN 978-1-63226-142-7
eBook ISBN 978-1-63226-143-4

PUBLISHED BY CREDENTIA PRESS
P.O. Box 3131
Westport, CT 06880
www.credentiapress.com

Book and cover design by Barbara Aronica
Art based on image from Shutterstock/Marish

Manufactured in the United States of America

I dedicate this book to a new generation of leaders who are entering the workforce with determination and curiosity; a new wave of catalysts embracing change to transform our future and reinvent the way we work; the trailblazers of the unknown whose courage and discernment are creating non-traditional pathways to success.

I am grateful and honored to have the opportunity to share what I've learned with you, the reader, whose consciousness will shape our collective wisdom. The seeds in this book are meant to be cultivated as a source of positive beliefs, collaborative connections, and creative expressions. Enjoy the experience!

CONTENTS

PREFACE

In most organizations, leadership development has been limited to a chosen few—high potentials, managers, or executives. But forward-thinking businesses today recognize the need to nurture leaders at all levels. The pioneers of a new leadership paradigm will shape organizational cultures and meet business challenges by sharing their social power equitably. Leadership isn't just about individual success—it's about boosting collective performance, enhancing customer and employee experiences, and driving tangible results. This book will guide you through your growth journey as you design your unique career path with confidence. The leadership skills I am sharing with you will prepare you for whatever path you choose in the ever-changing world of work. By trying out new ideas, connecting with a diverse network of professionals, and letting go of old assumptions, you will learn to be a high-performing team player. You will make a positive impact and collaborate in a way that aligns with your values, beliefs, work style, interests, and passions.

Discovering Your Potential

This book invites you to uncover what sets you apart from others in both your career and in your life. By activating your Personal Success Profile (PSP), you will develop the skills you need for a successful and fulfilling career. I will help you recognize your ever-evolving self and stay focused while you juggle other life commitments. The road to a balanced life isn't linear—it unfolds as you put the ideas from this book into action, shaping your identity beyond job titles. On these pages, you'll discover that self-acceptance is a crucial skill that will help you get rid of guilt, shame, and those pesky self-doubts that hold you back from becoming an awesome leader. To kickstart your growth journey, I'll ask you to dive into your work with robust enthusiasm, but avoid getting too emotionally attached to your projects and plans. Being engaged, yet not overly attached, lets you consider other people's ideas and perspectives and see opportunities you might've missed. Give it a shot today. It will open fresh perspectives on your role in the ever-evolving world of the social and professional communities where you are a cultural contributor.

As you shape your career in the workforce, you'll discover the leadership skills needed to guide yourself, others, and potentially, a whole organization in sync with the dynamics of the work landscape. One important skill we'll explore is Cognitive Mastery, which includes self-awareness. To bring your authentic self to the workplace, your career should align with your values and reflect your personality. It's also vital to embrace your imperfections—making you a well-rounded leader, no matter the setting. This work is rarely done within organizations, so it's up to you to strike a balance between personal and organizational goals as you plan your career path.

This process takes time—you can't rush it. It's all about quiet reflections and radical acceptance of who you are. You will be able to control and handle situations with more thought and less impulsiveness. Learning about the science behind behaviors, how people interact, and how personalities develop can shed light on your journey to becoming who you are today. By the time you finish reading this book, you will be able to show up at work with a strong sense of self and the confidence to unlock your full potential. It may seem like a big goal, but I know you can pave the way to an awesome career, with work-life balance to follow.

There are no short cuts to a balanced and fulfilling life. You'll need to practice staying in the moment, being present, and steering clear of distractions we often use to cope with tough thoughts and feelings. Feeling inadequate in new situations is okay—we're all human, after all. We're not that different, you and I. You can replace coping mechanisms such as drinking, binge-eating, or acting against your better judgment with positive behaviors. We all have our challenges, hidden sides, and flaws that might make us feel embarrassed, ashamed, or guilty. But on this journey, you'll realize that these feelings are normal, though they won't serve you well in the long run. Building your leadership skills takes courage to let go of old habits while respecting where you are in your personal growth and maturity.

As you dive deeper into this journey, you will need to ground yourself on some core principles. A basic one is that your experience of the world is shaped by the context and conditions of your emotional development. You've learned to cope, respond to the world, and react to perceived threats using available tools as you adapted in life. In other words, you've learned about trust, love, safety, and fear at a very young age, and developed a set of emotional reactions based on interactions with others and your perception of the world around you. You've acted according to how you were told to act, and built self-confidence based on the support you received from others. The great news is that you can now choose to build new habits and beliefs that can reduce anxiety, fears, and those self-limiting thoughts that so often hold you back from your dreams. It may seem hard to free yourself from negative beliefs about your abilities, but as you deconstruct your experiences in the workplace, you'll naturally notice the parallels between how you navigate your professional life and your personal experiences and societal influences. Essentially, our actions often reflect what we've absorbed from the messages, threats, rewards, and quality of interactions with the world around us.

You may see yourself as a complex person whose chances of changing are very low, but you are a dynamic individual, and your emotional intelligence is always evolving. Psychology has already mapped out ways for you to adopt new behaviors and better coping mechanisms. Neuroscience confirms that you can gradually create new pathways in your brain that allow you to respond to the world in fresh, realistic ways, and improve decision-making ability in key moments of your life. This is called "neuroplasticity," and research shows that your brain cells can reorganize their connections when you learn new coping skills and handle situations more effectively. It's like rewiring your brain, especially if you've been affected by traumatic events or developed certain thinking patterns to protect yourself from emotional pain. The first step is believing that you can do it, and the second step is staying focused. You will need to examine your current reactions and consciously find opportunities to process information in a less emotionally charged way. This means digging into the root causes of your impulsive reactions, which are usually deeply ingrained and may trigger challenging emotions. However, they also hold the key to healing from your past experiences.

The difficult part of this work is facing yourself without shame. Judgments seem to be everywhere. Looking at past behaviors and actions with guilt, shame, or regret will prevent you from seeing the situation objectively. Try to acknowledge the fact that most of what we do, think, and say, is driven by our complex minds. Bringing those unconscious patterns into our awareness is one of our goals in this learning process. The future will belong to those who can effectively collaborate with all kinds of people in the professional environment. Your overall experience will depend on your ability to discern between your reactions based on past experiences, preconceived notions about those different from you, and the opportunity to trust, respect, and learn from others when facing unexpected situations. As you engage in this process, new neuropathways will develop, allowing you to use cognitive and executive brain functions to respond appropriately to others and situations. Practicing with mindfulness is the best way to see events for what they are without letting our own limited perspectives color the picture.

Think back to when you had a negative reaction to a perceived change in your environment that was out of your control. How did you receive the news? Chances are, you made judgmental assumptions about why it happened, and who was to blame, even before you had the full story. It's totally natural to want to protect your comfort zone, especially if you've faced a lot of tough times in life. This reaction becomes your go-to response to a potential threat. But here's the thing: these knee-jerk reactions can't be ignored; they may not represent how you truly feel deep down. Stanford professor Carol Dweck breaks it down in her book *Mindset: The new Psychology of Success*. She talks about two basic approaches to life's changes and challenges. You can either have a fixed mindset, where you believe your capabilities and coping skills are set in stone, or you can embrace a growth mindset, with the belief you can adapt to change.

So far, we've introduced some ideas to help you make sense of what we call "coping mechanisms"—the ways in which people deal with life's challenges and threats. Over the past decade, loads of studies have confirmed that our early life experiences shape the defensive mechanisms that help us identify, react, and handle tough situations. In her book, Dweck states: "For twenty years, my research has shown that the view you adopt for yourself profoundly affects the way you lead your life." So, I invite you to explore a fluid understanding of your own beliefs, pre-programmed ways you've learned to see the world, and how you've developed your reactions to changes and threats. At work, how others perceive you becomes your reality. And guess what? Decisions are made emotionally more often than you might realize. Decisions about you, your career, and your potential to advance in the company, are usually discussed among leaders who observe you at work. As human beings, they might remember more vividly the times you didn't fully show up. Your reputation is vital in developing a successful career.

It is important to distinguish between the beliefs you've absorbed from others, values you've adopted due to peer pressure, friends, and the societal norms influencing your behaviors, and what resonates with you and represents who you are as a person. You will need to develop the ability to filter messages, data, and opinions, with a balance between your emotional reactions and knowing where your thoughts and feelings stem from. I get it—it can be exhausting, but here's the key: aim for progress, not perfection. Try this exercise: sit comfortably, close your eyes, and stay quiet for a few minutes. Breathe slowly, inflating your lungs from the diaphragm, the middle, and the upper torso. Hold the breath it for a second or two and then exhale for 5–7 seconds. Focus your mind on breathing. You can create a mantra and repeat it as you breathe: "I am learning, I have potential." Let thoughts come and go like clouds. Repeat this breathing exercise as it will help you center yourself in the moment. Being present is a skill you must develop as a leader. Sit with your eyes closed, breathe for a few minutes just experiencing the in and out of the air. Let go of all thoughts. Stay in quiet awareness. It is powerful.

In the workplace, mastering self-management is a must.

Most companies aim to build aspirational cultures that can sometimes clash with business priorities. In dynamic companies, situations like people leaving or new hires can shake things up. And sometimes, the great work you've done for your old boss may not be as relevant to the new boss. It is also possible that you didn't get the same opportunities as others to work on a high-profile project, or maybe your skills didn't match the available opportunities. Plus, most organizations are constantly changing at all levels. Either way, developing your leadership skills means diving into new abilities and daring to try new experiences, even when you're not completely sure you'll nail them.

You are already sensing that building a fulfilling career is not about perfection or following recipes to achieve predictable outcomes. It is about developing leadership skills from the start to stay focused on what truly matters. Your performance largely depends on your ability to collaborate with others and add value while also being open to others' input. You need to understand that organizations operate based on the beliefs and assumptions of their leaders. That's why it is important to learn how to assess situations, respond to them with a clear mind, and have the confidence to deal with self-limiting beliefs that get in the way.

I ask you to put aside your judgment, allow for new information to influence your thinking, and see the world through all the lenses that are available to you. Being present with an open mind allows your emotions to flow without overwhelming you. Seeing the world without fear is hard, but that's when you start building your true self. Being authentic is not about always reacting the same way. Authenticity comes from a clear understanding of your own values, principles, and beliefs that guide you even during difficult times.

Learning about your needs, naming your emotions, and communicating your intentions are as important as recognizing the needs of others and listening to them. Remember that the subtleties of your verbal and non-verbal messages play a role in how you're perceived. In your career, context can help you find new paths, bringing opportunities to express your aspirations with those who might be helpful to you. I am confident that you will soon see that letting go of your old attitudes about people and allowing for new experiences will bring you closer to your true self.

LEADING
TO
SUCCEED

CHAPTER 1

The Future of Work

Why should you care?

Expect rapid changes to continue in a world that's neither straight-forward nor linear. In today's economy, people are globally inter-connected, technology and innovation are driving new customer behaviors, and multiple forces are putting well established companies in competition with start-ups. The evolution of digital tools is changing the way we work. Options for workers are growing with the expansion of independent professionals seeking more autonomy and flexibility. The blend of remote and hybrid work models calls for better ways of working to boost performance. Regardless of your role in the Future of Work, you are a leader transforming the workplace in this collective movement. You'll have choices to make as an individual contributor, team member, leader, or executive in your work journey.

As an alternative to a full-time job, you may consider freelancing. You may also contemplate starting your own business. Regardless of the model of engagement you choose, take a moment to assess your ability to lead yourself, others and potentially a whole business. There are plenty of options, and your decision should be based on data, intu-ition, and above all, courage. Although these work models are flexible, and your circumstances may change, the way you choose to interact with others professionally is part of your profile as a leader. I have been an hourly worker in restaurants, full-time employee, an entrepreneur with a private practice, and returned to global companies to lead major missions and teams within the corporate context. It is possible to have a variety of experiences as you navigate your career. They all add value to your growth as a professional.

Leadership combines emotional development and cognitive abilities to help you assess situations. Recognizing that you are developing new skills will enhance your relationships outside of work as well. The flexibility you demonstrate navigating your conduct at work is part of how you build your reputation as a team member and as an expert. But do not forget to balance work with your own life.

Practice Mindfulness for better decision-making.

The world of work is reinventing itself at a rapid pace, and the playbook for success does not come with a manual on how to advance your career. That's why it is essential to develop lasting human skills that enable you to lead confidently and gracefully through uncertainty and ambiguity. You've probably heard of the power of mindfulness and meditation for decision making. This concept of making better decisions with a quiet mind and conscious reasoning works. Not convinced? Put it to practice: find a comfortable chair, don't cross your arms or legs, close your eyes, and focus on your breathing. Try to stay still, just observe the air when you inhale and exhale. Keep your eyes closed and take a deep breath, pause, and exhale fully. As your thoughts come to mind, see them as clouds in the sky, passing through. Focus on breathing again. Stay present. This exercise will have a calming effect. Keep going for about 3 minutes. Then recall a situation when you were confronted with an emotional trigger such as someone's complaint, or an event that made you react with anger. I am sure you were not thinking about your breath before you reacted, but that's a part of your training as a leader. It is a good start to learn to reflect and pinpoint your triggers. The practice is about being present in the moment, so you can reduce the reactive impulse and respond appropriately. You will make better decisions if you're calm and have the capacity to assess your options. Great leaders are not immune to emotional triggers, but they know to pause, breathe, and calmly respond within the context of the situation.

Being quiet, clearing your mind as much as you can, and focusing only on one thing—breathing—is a trick that can turn you into someone you truly admire. Learning these techniques takes time, and there may be moments when you're all jittery, struggling to concentrate, or just hitting a creative wall. It's in those offbeat moments when ingenuity can strike with unexpected ideas popping out of nowhere. Remember the saying "the best ideas happen in the shower?" Well, your greatest lightbulb moments might hit you during a break, a stroll, or when you're not even thinking about the topic at hand. That's why taking a mindful breathing break can do wonders. It's like hitting pause to unwind, finding some self-awareness, and letting tranquility guide you. This is also true for those tough talks with someone when you're not exactly feeling Zen about it. Regardless of how intense your feelings are, communication has to be a well-thought-out process that minimizes clashes, and amps up the chances of better results.

The transformation of the workplace is on-going.

The workplace is a complex environment, and you are the architect of your own experiences in a business culture that at times seems to be confusing and unorganized. But that's how companies are evolving in today's world. Remember, organizations are systems. They are complex, adaptable, dynamic, and often unpredictable. When you start a new job, you are expected to fit into the norms within the company's culture. Learn to adapt to new ways of working and show your personal qualities as well. Before we go deeper into your personal leadership development, we need to look at what's happening in organizations across the globe.

Businesses are evolving and becoming less hierarchical, less rigid, with new roles and more fluid job descriptions. When you plan your career, you will be confronted with the questions about what jobs to take, what industries to build your experience in, and what kind of format you want to build a career in. Senior leaders are realizing that they are underutilizing the skills of employees and overestimating the skills listed in job descriptions—creating frustrated employees. Organizational leaders are becoming attuned to the importance of building a diverse workforce for better decision making, better products and services, and an overall elevated culture that matches the demographic changes in their markets.

The success of these cultural transformations happening across all industries will vary from company size, history, and their leaders' willingness to take risks through experimenting and sharing of power. Like organisms, companies are always modifying operating models and adapting to world events to remain relevant. Forward-thinking organizations foster a culture of accountability by trusting cross-functional teams to work on complex issues and create innovative solutions for their customers. Intact teams working in isolation are no longer as effective as their multidisciplinary counterparts, and as a leader, you will need to build networked organizations with expertise. In this phase of the organizational revolution, it will be crucial that you rethink what you've learned in the past and allow for new perspectives to shape your ideas. The ability to be flexible, optimistic, and anticipate the future, will give you the freedom to explore options that were not available in the past.

Think about your own needs and how they are being met. What's missing in your work life today? Is your voice heard, respected, are your contributions rewarded? This is the basis of inclusive leadership that's increasingly more effective. Inclusive human-centric design is a next best practice, and it starts by focusing on those most impacted by what's being developed or planned. Employees at all grades may be included in designing initiatives, programs, and processes for the workforce of the future. User sponsors become integral in the ideation and design sprints, therefore programs and strategies are addressing their targeted population's needs and desires from the beginning of the process. Being inclusive requires you to think beyond the conventional frameworks to account for the diversity in the organization.

The world of work has been drastically impacted by global events and the only way forward is to design new organizations that place value in their people. Learning from and supporting each other, employees will define the greatest companies. If everyone is a leader, the organization becomes a network of experts and contributors who come together to collectively lead innovation, build better solutions, and enjoy more emotionally connecting experiences. Resulting in a fulfilling experience for each employee.

The work is also changing.

The work itself is another component of your leadership and career that needs to be scrutinized as you search for better ways to get things done. Most of the processes and organizing teams, functions, and departments have been designed in the last century. Informal and formal structures are designed to ensure lower risks and greater control over what's happening in the organization. Reporting teams and project management positions were very prominent until the emergence of Agile teams where leadership behaviors are expected from everyone, and daily practices create a dynamic workflow with an interactive approach to design, development, and deployment of products and services. Enabled by the digital transformation of the last twenty years, intelligent workflows and cross functioning teams are leading the way forward. Most enterprises embarked on the mission to rebuild their technology architecture, migrating their systems from on-site data centers to the hybrid cloud environment. IT architects and data scientists became central. Business leaders placed their bets that the data and insights derived from AI would provide them with an exponential competitive advantage.

Digital Fluency can't be underestimated in today's workplace. As an employee and as a leader, you must learn how to use digital tools to boost your performance and build social capital. Asynchronous work, collaboration in cross functional teams, and key contributions in a networked organization are often expected of you. Sharing expertise, knowledge, and ideas will be the way organizations promote high performance as we migrate evaluations and year-end assessments from individuals to teams.

The workplace is becoming more inclusive, offering equal opportunities for contributions from employees at all levels and backgrounds. Although most traditional enterprises today are struggling to harvest the best ideas and contributions from their employees, there is a strong movement toward sharing knowledge, and finding ways to express their ideas using omni channels of communication. Using LinkedIn to publish thought leadership is an example of how an individual might reach senior leaders in their own organization who are active members of the social media platform. In fact, in the future of work, sensing the opportunities, and acting with credibility and courage will become common place for leaders who know their value and are not afraid of expressing themselves. You are one of the pioneers of the new ways of working and leading. Take the stage and practice your leadership skills knowing you are making positive changes in the world.

It is important to note that your ability to influence others through storytelling and strong arguments will continue to be at the top of the list of leadership skills.

What are the main leadership skills? They include Cognitive Mastery, which helps you listen to others with attention, explore new solutions to challenges, and embrace a learning mindset with humility and curiosity towards diverse ideas. Another power skill is Adaptive Resilience which enables you to confidently navigate a dynamic organization within the hybrid work environment. Communicating across multi-channels and developing Digital Fluency will empower you for the future. Remember, asynchronous and distributed work will demand collaboration and empathy that will promote a more meaningful connection with coworkers.

Find and nurture mentors.

The best time to think differently and innovatively is now. Reinvent yourself by exploring new skills and seeking diverse perspectives to expand your knowledge—enhancing your opportunities for growth. While focusing on expertise and experiences, you will have to be more attuned to those around you to stay aligned. One way you can learn about your industry, your organization, and your professional community is by finding mentors to help you develop the required skills. One trick that always works is to offer a positive view of their contributions and how they are influencing you. Inclusive Interactions is a capability that covers relationship management. You can add it to your list of leadership skills. But to do it well, you must let go of what you want from others to start relationships that are more authentic and mutually beneficial.

You are now equipped to build a professional profile that catches the eye of hiring managers and other leaders in your industry.

Talent Marketplaces are becoming essential for finding the right talent needed in organizations, and you will greatly benefit from understanding how these platforms work. These AI-powered tools identify your skills based on your LinkedIn profile and resume. Providers of these services have access to vast amounts of data from the marketplace and the Internet, allowing them to improve their algorithms and offer platform members job recommendations, freelance opportunities, and learning experiences based on their skills. For modern professionals, the ability to build digital profiles, skills-based resumes, and use networking tools is a must. Your actions represent your ambitions, and in today's professional landscape, having a strong digital presence, and actively pursuing upskilling and reskilling is the norm.

What are your working preferences?

Take a moment to sit quietly and reflect on what kind of work truly excites you. Start by writing down your preferences for types of work that resonate with you. This is tricky as you might gravitate towards what you are used to doing, such as working on a project by yourself, playing video games in a competitive virtual environment, or playing team sports and so on. It is important to consider that however you decide to work, relationships are going to be part of your experience as a leader. Whether you are working independently or as part of a group, most of your customers, coworkers, partners, and team members will have their own styles and preferences. By allowing yourself to find productive ways to relate to different people, you can try new ways of communicating your ideas and choices as an adaptive behavior. Before asking people to understand your point of view, make sure you have expressed your understanding of their ideas first. Getting out of your comfort zone will always be a good practice in establishing your self-confidence.

Once you write a short paragraph about what kind of work suits your personality, preference, and purpose, you will understand yourself better. Are you leaning towards a job that will make money with no professional goal or aspiration? Try to find a root cause for the lack of aspiration. Is it a learned self-limiting belief about your lack of skills or capability? If so, use the breathing exercise to focus on your ability to learn, and let go of negative self-talk. In my twenty years of experience, I can positively affirm that all individuals have potential to reach their goals. If you are having a hard time recognizing your talent, the first question might be: Where and when did I start feeling this way? What have I internalized from others that led me here? Are there people in my life who believe in me? If you are comparing yourself to others on social media, you are doing a disservice to your self-esteem. Focus on your potential, trust that you have talent, and unique personal skills to make positive contributions to the world.

As you navigate this learning journey, you are already engaging in a process of Sense-Making, evaluating the context of your life, and most importantly, getting deep into the subconscious that shapes your values, ideas, passions, and desires. This kind of learning is a game-changer in your path to becoming a leader, and is your lifeline when you don't feel on top of your game. In fact, it is during tough times that leaders upskill—discovering things about yourself, learning to cope with emotions, and building resilience. Remember, there's nothing wrong with you if you can't figure everything out in one go. Allow for the process of exploration and self-awareness to take place without rejecting your thoughts and feelings. Sometimes the most important lessons will be learned during unpleasant experiences. We all have insecurities as professionals and as people, so don't deny yourself the chance to identify your fears and possibly, the irrational views you may be holding on to. Write them down and you will start experiencing the connection between thinking, writing, learning, and knowing thyself.

At this point, you might be questioning if leadership should be a priority when you aren't sure what kind of work you want to pursue. Keep your mind open and you will see the pathway before you. Don't force it. Lead yourself by knowing that you can count on people and other sources of knowledge that will help you see clearly. You might want to pursue a corporate job, or choose a small start-up. During the process, you will learn to listen to your intuition, combine it with data, and create a plan that may include being part of a team, taking on a business by yourself, or even becoming a freelancer who makes a living choosing projects, clients, and missions to work on independently. Work environments are changing rapidly, and your choices today may not dictate your whole career. Build confidence in your choices and your ability to develop a career that's satisfying and rewarding. But stick with leadership skills development to help you achieve your potential as you build your professional trajectory. It is an essential skill to cultivate from the start of your career.

Co-creating the future is an opportunity to lead.

Human curiosity and personal aspirations are intrinsic drivers of self-actualization—purpose and belonging—which are becoming performance essentials by the business community. Leaders in large organizations are talking about inclusion, partnerships, customers as co-creators, human-centered leadership, and the need for personalized employee experiences to drive a culture of high performance. Employees' well-being is now one of their top priorities. With increased access to information about their workforce, companies are committed to understanding their people better. However, personal experiences can't be fully determined by statistical reports or workforce analytics. Instead, employers need to rely on People Leaders with interpersonal skills to build trust, create a safe space for experiments and failure, as well as understand personal needs of employees without judgment. It's never too soon to learn to actively listen, be present, and share your expertise as you manage teams with a coaching approach.

People leaders of the future will co-create success by sharing decision-making power, accepting input from all team members, and building trust as a foundation for authentic relationships. And for that to happen, executive leaders, managers, and employees must achieve a level of respect for one another that goes beyond compliance. Creating and developing the workforce as a community of interdependent thinkers is only possible by integrating the personal and professional experiences of employees with a strong vision for the collective well-being of all members of the team. Through guiding and not ordering, you will lead the team toward high-value tasks, encourage self-determination among team members, and empower them to choose where and when they work. These shifts in workforce management and workplace norms will continue to transform the digital/physical environment of tomorrow. Creating a sense of closeness in a digital context while dealing with hybrid models will challenge organizations in the next decade. However, as the demand for specific skills grows, most organizations will be flexible about their employee locations to ensure they can attract and retain their top talent.

Design memorable experiences.

Design Thinking is widely used across industries to prioritize user experience over products as the main value driver. Professionals in User Experience (Ux) and Employee Experience (Ex) aim to create value by better understanding their users, using personas and inclusive processes that encourage exploration and innovation. Human Centered Design shares this belief, emphasizing value creation through creative practices aligned with the audience's needs. And finally, Inclusive Design speaks to the importance of diverse starting points for projects and products, ensuring relevance to a wide range of customers. To foster inclusive leadership, challenge your own beliefs and biases. Embrace new ideas and diverse perspectives, recognize the infinite potential in collective wisdom. Start innovation and initiatives by involving those who will be affected by your decisions and actions.

CHAPTER 2

Pioneering New Ways of Working

Embrace the power of a new generation of leaders.

In my experience in mental health, leadership development, consulting, coaching, HR executive roles, and thought leadership on the future of work, I've gained deep empathy for workers striving to balance the needs of their organizations, themselves, and society. My curiosity has led me to collaborate with brilliant minds in business to discuss disruptions in the workplace ecosystem. From activating major global transformations to intently listening to employees and innovators, I've grown convinced that low engagement, lack of strategic alignment, and overall dissatisfaction can be repaired by the adoption of a talent-development philosophy centered on leadership as a fundamental skill for all employees. Leadership isn't confined to the top ranks. It's a capability individuals can nurture to share power, model behavior with respect and dignity, and remain dedicated to collective purpose and inclusion.

Leadership is all about how leaders behave. Today's workplace is calling for a new kind of leadership that paves the way for a sustainable and more compassionate future. Employees are eager to play a larger role in decision-making, contributing innovative ideas, leading projects, and taking ownership of their work, regardless of their physical location or position in the organization. They aspire to be recognized for their ideas, skills, leadership potential, actions, and contributions. This sets the stage for the future of work: emotionally connected and empowered professionals who collaborate to tackle challenges for customers and colleagues. They learn from each other, support their teams, and establish a culture of trust and experimentation, allowing for risk-taking without fear of retribution. And ultimately, they're co-creating cultures that celebrate both failures and successes, while offering equal opportunities for career growth and skill development. In today's diverse and distributed workplace, everyone is a leader and has value, energy, and the ability to make a meaningful impact.

Leadership behavioral norms are shifting.

You've probably heard about the importance of using data for decision-making, and relying on science for more objective opinions. I appreciate the value of data, and I won't inundate you with studies and research showing the well-known issues we face in organizations today. You can easily find studies on almost any topic you're interested in by searching online or asking a Gen AI app. Every entity involved in data collection, survey deployment, and insight analysis has published reports claiming to be "research" based. But the reality is that most surveys and responses are not analyzed within the context of each respondent. It is crucial that you develop critical thinking to interpret the information around you and make sense of it independently. In the modern workplace, everyone should be interested in solving the human capital challenges that affect the bottom line. Business success results from having a clear strategy and self-directed teams committed to acting with agility and decisiveness. This approach fosters a high-performance culture that transcends functional and business group boundaries.

To achieve radical change within an organization and impact its way of functioning, it's important to avoid blaming specific groups within the organization. Blame only perpetuates the issues that have been growing in modern society for some time. Instead, I encourage you to practice what I call "Emotional Attunement" by understanding others, even when their opinions differ from your own. For some leaders, the goal is to maintain a sense of control during uncertain times. Avoid self-righteous behaviors when dealing with multiple viewpoints, and it will help you focus on challenges with objectivity and openness. This, in turn, can lead to creative solutions for business challenges.

You can start by fostering an environment where issues can be openly discussed, without immediately dismissing others' perspectives or devaluing them. In diverse organizations, we have members with unique experiences and ideas. Listening to them all is crucial for creating plans that align with your company's purpose and strategy, while also instilling a strong belief in the collective power of people working together on innovative solutions. With your skills, you can create a space where employees' individual experiences and aspirations can align with a fair and inclusive workplace that offers opportunities for all. It doesn't matter where you are in the organization, you can nurture leadership skills and inspire others to work toward a better tomorrow. However, this style of leadership, which involves leading yourself, others, and the organization, requires a certain level of awareness that takes time and effort to develop.

As you prepare to become a leader of the future, you will need to assess your own interests while considering the needs of the entire workforce and the business you're committed to. Stay humble in your assumptions to avoid letting your unconscious biases influence your decisions and actions. If the workplace is to become a powerhouse of skills, capabilities, and innovation for everyone, employees should be encouraged to experiment, develop a sense of agency, and receive support as they explore new paths. They must also feel psychologically safe for open and healthy communication, leading to fantastic ideas. Remember, some of the most impactful moments for employees involve leaders displaying vulnerability, sharing with no judgment, and expressing humility. You might recall a time when a leader's authenticity and courage made you feel a profound sense of connection. Those moments are priceless and incredibly motivating.

The workplace is where you can step out of your comfort zone and push yourself to become even better. It's all about experimenting, embracing failure without shame, and putting your well-being first. With each lesson, you build resilience and leadership skills for the future.

Navigate the Imposter Syndrome.

The Imposter Syndrome manifests itself when you feel like you are unqualified for your job title and will be discovered as a fraud. But if you ask yourself the following question, you will realize that Imposter Syndrome is a normal reaction to new situations and experiences. The question is: How can you advance in your career if you are not placed in challenging new roles? Believe in your ability to learn and overcome the syndrome. It's okay to have doubts when you're trying something new, as long as it doesn't hold you back. As a leader, your role is to acknowledge and share things. Here's a tip: self-confidence isn't about knowing everything—it's about believing you can learn, and that you have every right to be where you are. You may not know something yet, but with curiosity and willingness to learn, you'll get there.

As you explore your leadership potential, you will face risks, adversity, and the temptation to express your anxiety and uncomfortable experiences in unhealthy ways. An important attribute of great leaders is the ability to remain calm, reflect on difficult situations and discern actual feelings and emotions. The healthier way to manage uncomfortable feelings is to use what in psychology is called "adaptive coping skills." These may include therapy, exercise, talking to a trusted friend, or any activity that may reduce your anxiety and stress levels. Practicing mindfulness, meditation, and reflection will help you remain centered under pressure. Focus on progress, not perfection.

When you think about an organization you would like to join, how do you decide if it's the right fit for you? This is an important question as you shape your career and understand your own needs and biases. This is a good time to ask yourself what really matters the most to you in a work environment. What's acceptable and what may present a challenge for you? Sometimes you will need to allow for compromises that can help you gain the experiences you'll use down the line. If you are interested in learning more about a given industry, you might need to become an employee within it—to try new experiences.

To develop Adaptive Resilience as a professional, make sure you have a self-care plan. Being reactive usually makes the problem worse, so instead, step back, take a break, reframe the problem into something that can be dealt with in a collaborative effort or whatever fits the situation. Approach each situation with a fresh perspective and try not to pile up on past experiences, as this approach will soon mentally exhaust you.

Leadership has been defined in many ways over the years, and there are thousands of models, approaches, and frameworks available. What I am suggesting is a fresh perspective on evolution in how we think about leadership in today's ever-changing work landscape. In this context, leadership is about putting energy into action. Leadership is an adaptive way of thinking that aligns with how people want to lead and be led. Gone are the days of old-school management and rigid hierarchies. In this world of constant change and adaptation, the winners will be those who stay engaged, know who they are, are curious about what's possible, and have the courage to act decisively and swiftly.

Democratization of leadership means senior leaders sharing power with those that are worthy of the responsibility. Consciousness, Curiosity, and Courage drive the new workplace culture. As a pioneer, you can revolutionize how organizations function, how employees are led, and how the workflow is reimagined. To make it happen, you will need to start reshaping your leadership skills and be prepared for bigger responsibilities.

Talent characteristics shaping the future of work.

The Five Ds of the new workforce
Distributed
Dynamic
Digital
Diverse
Discerning

The new workforce is distinguishing itself with five traits that have emerged from macro and micro changes in the business world today.

1. Distributed

The first characteristic of the workforce may not fully apply to all types of work, as most frontline employees need to show up to work in person. The rise of remote-first organizations combined with the advances in technology, is paving the way for the emergence of Virtual Enterprises by 2030. When it comes to choosing between work formats—on-site, remote, or hybrid—some organizations are sticking with what's familiar, others are applying a flexibility that's causing more confusion than freedom, and still other organizations are listening to their employees and customers to find a balance.

The workforce is changing, and forward-thinking companies are getting ready for a more distributed multi-generational workforce. Skills scarcity is reshaping hiring practices, making remote work a growing trend. And remember, careers are non-linear and there is no harm in course correcting as you go.

For some, working from home is a great option if they are dealing with caring for an elderly parent or a child, allowing them to have a full-time job while staying at home. Others strive for physical contact with their peers. But this dilemma doesn't have to be binary—the world of work will keep changing, and new ways of organizing work process will emerge. Companies can transform offices into community hubs and host meaningful events to keep their culture alive. There will be new ways of thinking about community building and performance. It's all about staying open-minded in the changing world of work.

2. Dynamic

The dynamic workforce reflects a common trend among young professionals. They aim to boost their careers, gain fresh experiences, and sometimes increase earnings by switching jobs. The phenomenon is not new: millennials started a trend highlighting that staying in the same job for more than a few years may hinder advancement. Remember, there is no right or wrong answer when it comes to changing jobs. Your success will depend on factors like skill growth, professional reputation, and access to opportunities at your current job. Your success is a shared responsibility between you and your employer.

The dynamic workforce is reshaping how companies manage their people, and you will not only be living this transformation, but will be a part of the solution. The discovery of new ways of working includes gig projects, team-based missions, and a concept penned by John Boudreau: "work without jobs." In this context, dynamism applies not only to career pace, but to how work gets done. It is an exciting era where everyone is a leader, and innovative ideas are collectively developed and adopted within adaptive organizations.

As you reinvent your leadership journey, it will be important to explore your current personal beliefs instilled by your parents, teachers, and friends. You'll find that old concepts are influencing your actions in ways that aren't aligned with who you are today. As you may have already noticed, leadership development is complex, mirroring the diverse worldviews of society. It is the role of the leader to assess context, acknowledge reality, and embrace new ways of learning from multiple sources to achieve business results, and foster an inclusive and equitable organizational ecosystem.

As a member of the workforce, you are shaping the future and influencing others. Developing leadership skills early on is key. It means listening to your environment, thinking creatively, and adapting to new challenges. Your success relies on learning from experiences, aligning your goals with the team, and seeking support from your network.

3. Diverse

Diversity is a core belief driving organizational value. Inclusive leadership shapes every aspect of a company, from hiring to promoting. Most companies are not there yet, and you can pioneer this inclusive mindset. It is not an exercise of the mind, but an openness of your heart that will allow you to see the value in every single person. And being attuned to individuals of diverse and historically discriminated groups, you too will be a catalyst of change.

Inclusion does not discriminate.

Regardless of who you are, you belong here. You are a member of the working community, responsible for its collective well-being, and you play a vital role in shaping our workplace culture. Culture is dynamic and evolves with each action of individuals like yourself. Contrary to what you have heard in the past, preserving the status quo isn't sustainable. As you develop your leadership skills, you will face some uncomfortable truths about yourself and others that will help you mature. Trust the process of growth, be curious about others, and stay open to diverse perspectives. But of course, this takes time and courage to examine how the status quo has been established. As a leader, you're a pioneer in creating a more transparent workplace.

The secret is to lead in a state of abundance, where everyone can contribute, and all voices are heard. Great leaders embrace diversity as a source of strength in a high-performing culture. They are self-aware, recognizing their beliefs, potential, and flaws—driving them to learn and grow. You, as a wise leader, will understand historical inequalities, challenge harmful practices, and champion inclusivity for a more fair workplace. The demographics of the world are shifting, bringing diverse talent and perspectives that enrich organizations aiming for sustainability. Be the leader you admire!

4. Digital

Digital skills are vital for a high-performing workforce. Being adept with apps, collaboration tools, and data systems sets you apart as a leader. Navigating the workplace demands structured thinking and organizational skills to drive projects and teams toward success. When managing complex initiatives, consider using Agile tools and digital design thinking for ideation, defining goals, and creating MVPs with an inclusive team. Your success relies on sharing knowledge in a digital environment, especially in distributed, fractional, or cross-functional teams. Digital natives are comfortable interacting virtually, but building connections in the digital world may not be as easy for other people.

The risk of alienating team members is high in multi-generational workplaces. Leaders should educate, not embarrass others for their lack of knowledge. Remember how you felt when you didn't know what others did? It does not foster inclusion and can hinder the work across team members with complementary skills. As a conscious leader, avoid using your knowledge to exert power. Everyone has the potential to learn and lead. If you keep that in mind, you will be more effective in creating collective value, and enhancing your team's skills, leading to better results.

As a digital leader, find your own network of knowledge workers to explore the potential of the digital workplace. Encourage teams, colleagues, and hesitant leaders to experiment. Sharing your own journey can inspire others to overcome their digital fears. To engage a multigenerational workforce, create reverse mentoring teams to bridge the digital generation gap.

5. Discerning

The modern workforce, shaped by the chaos of the twenty-first century, is changing how organizations operate. Employees are no longer blindly following traditional career paths. They've seen pay disparities, start-up disruptions, and job insecurity. Today's workers are smartly evaluating their career options as they're no longer limited to traditional full-time roles. The open economy, flexible talent pools, and post-industrial work landscape are redefining power balance between employers, employees, and independent workers globally.

External motivators may not be the best predictors of success. Look within: it's about what you want and are willing to pursue that will define your path. Some of the most successful leaders took unconventional routes. How you choose to express yourself can inspire others—leading to a more diverse and flexible workforce structure.

There is a new awareness among the workforce, questioning traditional work setups and hierarchies. Many are rethinking their retirement plans, career paths, and the trade-offs they're unwilling to make to titles or power. This is a great chance for you to redefine work in the twenty-first century. Your ability to sense what's happening in the world of work, analyze career paths of previous generations, and build your own working experience are crucial to your success.

CHAPTER 3

The Road to Awareness, Acceptance, and Action

Every encounter is an opportunity to learn.

In my own personal journey as a Latino immigrant who came to the US with no English, little money, and no social support, I can assure you that it all depends on how you use your creativity, expertise, and life skills. Being optimistic and envisioning a better future is crucial. I started my life in the US after earning a degree in communications in Brazil. At first, I couldn't find work with my poor knowledge of English. I became a busboy in a restaurant where most servers and managers made fun of my language skills. Although it was a hurtful experience, I kept trying to learn the language by attending free ESL classes and adapting to the new environment. This initial experience in the US helped me become a more inclusive leader, with empathy for those who are struggling in life due to socially-constructed obstacles.

If you are a member of a minority or underserved group, negative memories and awareness of inequality can impact your job searches and confidence in interviews. However, when you see your life experiences as valuable skills beyond your technical expertise, you begin the journey to radical acceptance and empowerment. These skills build character and allow you to apply creativity, empathy, and adaptability in your career. Focus on what you've learned outside your formal education to build your leadership brand with confidence. When you share your challenges with your peers, something special happens: resonance, which creates a beautiful connection with others.

A leader stays in the present, understands others without judging, and focuses on what's important. They connect emotionally, build trust, and create memorable moments that become cultural milestones. Beyond technical skills, great leaders embrace inclusivity, learning from all backgrounds and career stages. The next-gen leaders are building their personal brand with their own world view, new expectations and needs. You can do the same by considering all your experiences as learning opportunities. The ability to stay confident and resilient during tough times will define your leadership style and reputation. Being vulnerable with others creates the psychological safety that supports high-performing teams.

Here's a story that might inspire you. Opportunities in life depend on your proactive approach, creativity, resilience, and willingness to take risks. After running my psychotherapy private practice, executive coaching, and HR/Leadership consulting for almost four years, my husband and I moved away from New York City. I felt the need for experience in a large global firm. That's when I realized that a large tech company had its headquarters near my new home, and I decided to secure an interview. When I called the Talent and Diversity leader, his assistant refused to connect me. Instead of giving up, I tried to guess his email address using the company's format. I sat at my kitchen table with pen and paper in hand and started to play with combinations of his name. First initial, dot, last name, then last name followed by first name and ended up with fifteen combinations. I sent a simple message to them all, expressing my admiration for the company's values and my desire to contribute. To my surprise, the busy leader replied that he forwarded my resume to HR.

During the first interview with HR, they questioned my lack of large organization experience. I responded by emphasizing my belief in their values and how I could champion their culture. In about a month

I had an offer to become an Executive and Organizational Leadership Consultant. Starting in this corporate role, I knew there was much to learn. I used my social skills to build relationships and navigate the academic aspects of the job. This experience was challenging, and I was the only minority with an accent, so an Imposter Syndrome was inevitable. But I realized that this reaction was normal, and my experiences and qualifications would help me build my expertise and confidence. I approached the group with a positive attitude, empathy, and willingness to collaborate, which left a strong impression.

These challenges I'm sharing reflect my journey into a new career in the global business world. It's about being willing to pursue opportunities that may seem out of reach, growing your skills, confidence, and curiosity along the way. One important insight for your career: believe in yourself. You have the permission to explore, learn, expand your horizons, and spread your wings. Self-limiting thoughts and judgment may paralyze you, but recognizing and managing them is part of your Cognitive Mastery, another powerful skill. Social barriers can be tough, but they're part of your life's journey. Shed the negative perceptions, let go of doubts, and embrace self-acceptance. Start this transformation now! Ready?

Enter the journey with compassion.

Exploring your beliefs and values, and fully accepting yourself, helps you develop coping skills to navigate life at work and at home. By reflecting on your behaviors, habits, and attitudes, you can trace how life events, family dynamics, and your environment influenced your responses over time. Psychology, psychotherapy, behavioral science, and more recently neuroscience, are shedding light on how our biological makeup and emotional development interactions with our childhood caretakers, have contributed to forming our personality and beliefs system. It sounds complex but take a moment to look at your history with compassion for yourself and others. To start developing your awareness and acceptance, you might want to sit still, close your eyes, breathe deeply and slowly while reflecting on one positive belief about yourself. Stay in that space, even if your family and friends don't share this belief. Find the courage to love yourself without judging, accepting who you are with kindness.

Regardless of your history, you can change how you think and react to life's ups and downs. Being mindful and challenging negative self-perceptions helps you find your true self and discover the authentic leader within. I mentioned self-limiting beliefs a few times, and it is important to understand them. I worked hard to overcome one of my own, which was that as an immigrant I wouldn't reach leadership positions due to my education background. Another limiting belief was about being an immigrant with a heavy accent—I feared it would hinder my career. Overcoming these beliefs takes reflection and talking about them. You've created them to protect yourself and maintain a sense of control, even when that choice was limiting your potential. Neuroscience shows our brains are sensitive to perceived threats, which trigger negative reactions to challenges and past traumas.

Wisdom whispers when you least expect it, and often when you are not ready to listen.

How you react to perceived threats can reveal your learned emotional reactions. With some reflection, you change how you handle triggering events in a better way. This is an invitation to discover new, positive ways of assessing situations and people in your life. Most of your decisions are driven by emotions and unconscious processes. Memories can be powerful, but remember, you've already overcome life's toughest moments, thanks to your inner strength. Unfortunately, traumas are part of life, and they can often overshadow your thoughts and leave lasting marks. Paradoxically, these difficult moments offer a chance to redefine yourself. You can separate these events and those who hurt you from who you are today. While therapy with professionals can be quite helpful, you can also uncover and reorganize memories through self-reflection, developing healthier coping skills for your physical and emotional health. This is how you enter the realm of consciousness and connect with your spiritual, emotional, and social aspects of self.

Energy is your natural resource.

Meditation can be a good way to start this journey, and though progress is gradual, it's worth the effort. Being present, breathing with the intention of letting go of your thoughts, can help clear your crowded mind. Staying focused, can bring peace and clarity and help you interact with others without emotionally charged reactions. This is especially useful at work, whether you're starting a new job, joining a team, or meeting coworkers for the first time. Stay present in the moment to ground and boost your confidence. And remember, you don't need to be perfect to be yourself, and being engaged without being too attached allows new ideas to shape better outcomes.

In my early years as a social worker, I felt comfortable sharing my experiences as a Latino immigrant in New York City. But as a consultant to corporate organizations, I avoided personal disclosures, especially with executive leaders, when triggered by a perceived threat. It was awkward to sit in a meeting with executives sharing experiences I couldn't relate to. My accent made me stand out, and I felt shame for not understanding cultural references. These reactions were natural, but unproductive. Over time, I learned to trust my self-worth, let go of my old reactions and take agency over my actions. It's a gradual process but taking risks can lead to positive outcomes.

You may be reluctant to reveal your identity to strangers as you don't know how they'll react. But as you build a support system and the courage to be authentic, you can shape your future differently. As a leader, you should learn to recognize and understand people, even those who you may subconsciously perceive to be a threat. This involves developing the ability to assess situations and meeting people different from you without judgment, which can be tough if you have never questioned your beliefs. You likely have some biases, preconceived ideas, and binary opinions, and to let go of them requires self-exploration and curiosity about others. The road to self-discovery is non-linear and ongoing, but it's the path of becoming someone you respect, admire, and love. And self-acceptance is the key to becoming your best self.

Leading yourself to become who you want to be.

Leading yourself consciously is a prerequisite to leading others and organizations. Regardless of your workplace environment, your success can't be dependent on your skills and expertise alone. As the workplace changes, professionals and team members are recognizing the value of leadership skills. Self-awareness, agility, flexibility, collaboration, cognitive mastery, and emotional intelligence are essential skills for all professionals. Seeking honest feedback from others can help you challenge your perspectives and adopt new knowledge. By allowing your opinions, assumptions, and biases to transform into balanced reasoning you'll support collective goals and enhance your professional image. Developing resilience, slowing your reactive impulses, and navigating complex workplace situations differentiates you from others who have similar expertise, but may lack in emotional literacy.

A personalized approach to learning, living, and leading becomes a journey into consciousness, curiosity, and courage.

As previously mentioned, we manage life stressors in two ways: When unable to assess the risks and long-term impact of adverse events, we react in self-preservation mode and make impulsive decisions. Our brains can go into "fight or flight" modes when external stimuli cause "emotional hijacking." This state prevents us from reflecting and applying reason before reacting based on emotions. This is common for those who've had early adverse experiences and formed a quick reaction to avoid suffering and pain. Our brains are wired this way, with the emotional center in the brain called the amygdala often being hypervigilant and overriding logical processes. It's important to understand your triggers and learn to respond calmly. A second way we can manage our stressors is by using adaptive coping skills and approaching situations by recognizing emotional reactions and using our cognitive capabilities to respond more effectively.

Between stimulus and our response there is a space. In that space is our power to choose our response. In our response lies our growth and our freedom. –Viktor Frankl, the Austrian psychiatrist who founded logotherapy.

To develop adaptive coping skills, practice some self-love. Remember, neuroplasticity allows us to create new neural pathways through focus, practice, and optimistic approach to life. Be present, choose love and dive into the unknown with compassion for yourself and others. The workplace is evolving to value emotional well-being, so start working on yourself by journaling, meditating, or simply taking time to think before reacting to conflict or stress.

I had no support system when I came to the US, and often coped by reacting impulsively to avoid emotional distress. The key is not to judge yourself for not instantly changing old patterns. Allow for compassion and forgiveness towards yourself, always. Have courage to see events objectively, explore your history, believe in your potential, and recognize your inner light that transcends time and space.

Learning about maladaptive and adaptive coping mechanisms is just one way to see and accept your own responses without shame. Meditation can be very productive if you allow for self-acceptance. Remind yourself that you live in a world that contributes greatly to negative judgments and self-talk. Just take a minute to think about the last twenty-four hours. How many times did you check your social media profiles? What drove you to do so? Were you seeking validation, recognition, connection? Whatever you find yourself lacking is a direct result of the relationships you developed with others, including family. Supportive people in your life understand that constructive feedback and reassurance of love is integral in the development of your self-esteem and emotional health. But most people had their share of adversity in life and have to rely on their own conscious effort to work on themselves. Besides, there will always be people on your path who project their issues onto you and call it feedback. It is at your discernment to know whose words to take to heart.

When you're on social platforms, you often act subconsciously. It's been well documented that most of our actions are driven by our emotions, so it's natural to experience anxiety, frustration, sadness, and loneliness at times. Scrolling on social media may give you a temporary gratification, but don't rely on it too much. Break the cycle, create your own freedom, and embrace your fabulous authentic self. This is how you can build a career path that's non-conventional, yet successful.

Don't worry if you're not your best self yet; I'm not here to turn you into a superhero. Instead, I will tell you that you can, and you will learn how to lead yourself, manage your emotions, think with clarity, and most of all, find happiness within yourself, and on your own terms. Life shines from within, and you will find the hidden beauty in the most difficult times in your life. As an explorer of the future, you must look at things without analyzing them too soon. Be curious.

You know now that you make judgments to protect yourself from threats, but those are inherent survival mechanisms from our ancestors, and it is up to you to learn new ways of seeing the world. The first steps are not easy. Seeing the world with "soft eyes" and responding to stimuli with grace will improve your reputation as a professional and a leader. "Soft eyes" allow you to see what's around you using peripheral vision to better sense your environment. The narrower your focus, the more limited your view. Choose a panoramic style of seeing the world instead of trying to zoom in.

CHAPTER 4

Distributed Power for Distributed Teams

Leadership is everyone's business.

Power is something you must understand, generate, embrace, share, and use in service of the collective. In the modern workplace, we must rethink power beyond titles and hierarchies that slow things down. We need to shift from the concept of personal power to that of the collective, and develop a clear purpose, focused on strategic goals. Most organizations still use outdated decision-making models, but it's time to adopt dynamic systems. But before we delve into organizational leadership, we must recognize that all employees will be leading in some capacity, even when in individual contributor roles. I believe that in the future, everyone should have access to power and leadership as tools to perform at their best.

You've got what it takes to become your best self by practicing healthy habits. Start by envisioning who you want to become without being too critical. Take a moment to complete this sentence: "I aspire to become . . ." Let go of past attachments and simply let your thoughts flow. This exercise helps open your heart, connect with your authentic desires, and see if your choices align with your true self. This exercise can also be helpful when you encounter an annoying person or situation. Pema Chodron, a Buddhist monk, stated that being angry is usually fueled by a loop that involves at least one other person. She recommends trying to recognize the loop quickly and not let it turn into a spiral.

Coming from a family with limited resources, I grew up with the goal of making enough money so I could avoid financial struggles. Yes, I did manage to support myself once I came to the US, but it wasn't necessarily the most exciting aspiration to become a busboy in a restaurant. The desire to help others develop coping skills, and challenging my own limiting beliefs became my purpose through a lot of reflection. In fact, success happened when my focus shifted to helping create inclusive workplaces where everyone could shine. Learning about diversity and inclusion made me a stronger advocate for personal power. It was through self-reflection that I found the unlimited sources of positive energy we can tap into when we break free from emotional constraints and self-criticism. Allow yourself to see what value others bring to the collective consciousness and challenge your bias and judgments. Our humanity thrives when we bring out the best in ourselves and each other.

Tap into your power by setting ambitious aspirations. Leadership is becoming essential as work structures shift toward more shared power and common goals. Shared leadership and power create inclusive, innovative, and fulfilling working culture. Through daily intentional interactions with others and your ability to see yourself objectively, you can build confidence and a unique personal brand. Your value as a leader is in your ability to radiate positive energy, champion others' ideas, and promote equal opportunities for career growth. Your success comes naturally when you let go of trying to compete. In fact, for a leader, success happens when others recognize your power to be humble, approach situations with humility, and retain curiosity about others with generosity and interest. Succeed by sharing your time, knowledge, experiences, and vulnerabilities with others.

Lead in the new workplace.

Workplace culture greatly influences who becomes successful in an organization. In a traditional business, senior executives use the hierarchical system, which leads to perfectionism, fear of failure, and fragmented teams. This faulty mindset focuses on the business as an orderly set of skills, tools, and technology that prioritizes profits over progress, and processes over people. In setups like these, people are not practicing radical collaboration, nor celebrating breakthroughs in their collective efforts. Furthermore, these businesses are not building healthy and sustainable cultures. On the other hand, progressive and innovative companies are applying the newest knowledge, experimenting, and focusing on doing things better, not perfectly. These are workplaces where positive culture is palpable, and it reflects in the energy of the teams working together. This is the organization of the future you want to prepare yourself for.

As you step into the business world, be ready for challenges and the influence of others. Embrace unexpected opportunities and projects to develop the necessary leadership skills for the evolving era of Human Capital Management. Stay curious, free yourself from the old rules, and collaborate with others who share your enthusiasm for shaping the future. You're a part of a new workforce that's comprising the next generation agile enterprise and moving to OKR (Objectives and Key Results) instead of focusing on the static and rigid KPI (Key performance indicators). It may sound like a detail in the overall organizational system, but verbalizing aspects of work in the most dynamic and simplest ways will better your chances of success in creating a more inclusive future of work.

The future belongs to teams that work together toward common goals, while respecting each team member's uniqueness and considering the needs of their customers and end users. In any organized group of people, from families to social clubs, to support groups, to workplace teams, you might notice that past experiences influence your interactions today. Think about the roles you played in your family—caretaker, the doer, the handler, the smart one, the rebel, the shy and quiet one, and so on. Now think back to other groups you joined in school and maybe work; you will find that the people who caused you harm in the past are probably represented in some shape or form in your current environment. For example, if you had an aunt who always made fun of you, jokes from a female team member will likely irritate you. An authoritarian manager who does not listen to you might remind you of a father figure you had a hard time communicating with. Don't worry, you are not alone. Understanding these triggers can help you approach people with curiosity, seeing them objectively and learning new ways to interact.

Teamwork is all about embracing each other's differences, styles, and ways of expression to achieve a common goal. Teams can teach you about your own interpersonal issues. The good news is that when you are a member of an effective team, you will be able to work through your challenges. Teams hold a lot of value in organizations, and all members of a team need leadership skills to lead themselves with respect, and let everyone's best performance flow. Healthy teams openly discuss their work, prioritize tasks, make decisions together, and address issues as they arise. This approach fosters psychological safety and reduces resistance.

Developing leadership skills means challenging your opinions and beliefs for success in the communities you're a part of. Leadership is about trust, integrity, intention and support. Diversify your network to engage in diverse discussions and expand your perspectives. This will help you become less fixated on your own ideas, allow your ego to not depend on your need to be right, own the room, or be the center of attention. Trust the team process, use strategic inquiry to make informed decisions and encourage a culture of team recognition before individual recognition. As you create better experiences for all, you'll deliver valuable outcomes for the team and organization.

Team success is the goal, but don't forget the importance of personal recognition for your professional growth. These moments define your reputation. When you are "seen" as a leader, share the recognition with your team. You might say: "I am thrilled with the results our team accomplished on this project," or state that you enjoyed working with this team that inspired you to bring your A-game. Leaders don't take full credit for any of their wins! Your humility will create trust and attract skilled colleagues. Learn to motivate, course correct, and engage people for better outcomes. Focus on group recognition, and when discussing your accomplishments with your manager, offer solutions for strategic priorities of the business. If complimented, just be graceful and say thank you.

As a leader, be open to continuous learning, identifying skills and abilities for your growth beyond your current role. Differentiate yourself by taking risks, detours, and alternate routes to success. Amazing career experiences sometimes lie off the main highway. A well-developed leader can navigate ambiguity and uncertainty with optimism, going step by step, even when the outcome isn't clear. Trusting yourself is easier when you have worked on self-acceptance and self-awareness. And that's why we will explore the cluster of skills that align with your aspirations. A good exercise is to describe yourself in the third person, detaching from your own thoughts. Start describing a leader you admire and want to follow.

Stay present, embrace life without judgment, and manifest love to nurture your Consciousness, Curiosity, and Courage. To help you prepare for the future of leadership, let's rethink it. Leadership has been explored for decades, and thousands of books have been published on the subject, but the new paradigm in business requires a new mindset for dealing with multiple contexts, customers, and transforming industries. Your leadership shines when you stay calm, empathize with others, and lead with a clear vision. Explore the psychological concept of "projection" which is a defensive mechanism we use for unconscious emotions that may be difficult to accept, so we assign them to someone else. If I am unable to accept the fact that I am a competitive person, I might assign this characteristic to someone else as a judgment of their character. If I believe being competitive is a negative trait, then it's easier to project it onto others than face it myself. Projection also completes the picture of a person when we don't know them well. If I admire someone's success and don't know what it had cost them, I might project my own ideals onto them. I used to think that great leaders were immune to bad moods, self-limiting beliefs, feeling inadequate, and so on, but those were my own projections when I didn't know better. As I matured, I've learned to see leaders more and respect them. Normalizing our experiences helps us use less projection, and nurture self-acceptance instead.

It may sound paradoxical, but today's successful leaders need to let go of their own opinions and expert views to navigate the emerging business landscape with creativity. I've been observing leaders all over the world for over twenty years, and it's clear we're entering uncharted leadership territory. In the early twenty-first century, we admired leaders who had global mindset business expertise. They needed an Ivy League education and international credentials to reach the C-suite.

Leadership meant individual competence in managing, influencing, and growing the business. They were seen as superhumans in prestigious roles. But the context changed rapidly with the globalization of markets, technology, start-ups, and new customer behaviors. Companies embraced digital transformation, introduced new products and services, and met employee demands for meaningful work and flexibility. Leadership is evolving towards distributed power and shared leadership as the default in thriving organizations.

Shared leadership is changing modern businesses by breaking down hierarchical structures. Organizations are dynamic and complex systems, adapting to external and internal disruptions, from changing markets to social media challenges. Leaders are now challenged with added responsibilities of addressing racial equity and Environment, Social, and Governance (ESG) concerns. In today's environment, a leader must be curious about their constituents' concerns and expectations. And that's why today, many companies are adopting the idea that all employees are leaders, accountable for their careers and the organization's well-being. This shift impacts learning strategies, career development, and encourages senior leaders to share power. It also empowers employees to become ambassadors for their organizations across the markets they compete in.

Your leadership skills will help you navigate volatility, uncertainty, and the constant changes in organizations. Markets face supply chain issues, employee turnover, global health crises, and climate change, to name a few. Skills scarcity is hindering companies' strategies, so employers are leveraging everyone's strengths and leveraging overall growth over individual interests. I've observed organizations aligning their values, beliefs, and actions to meet customer needs. Leading cross-functional collaboration can be difficult to orchestrate, and top executives are expanding their roles beyond traditional control and operations. In the modern workplace, business knowledge is essential, but it's not enough. Social capital, your ability to connect and collaborate, is the real measure of your value.

Leadership is a powerful driver of success and innovation. It thrives on inclusive teams that co-create better outcomes. Forward-thinking leaders share power and are empathetic to those with valuable ideas who may fear rejection. Future leaders act as translators, helping teams align with dynamic strategies by understanding environmental influences. They stay attentive to signals for emerging trends, changes, and opportunities, integrating high volumes of data and remaining resilient. If you aspire to become a leader, start by listening to your thoughts, challenging your pre-conceived ideas, and welcoming others' contributions. Becoming a great leader is about becoming a great human being.

CHAPTER 5

Leadership Expression: Consciousness = Being

Manifest your human capabilities to thrive.

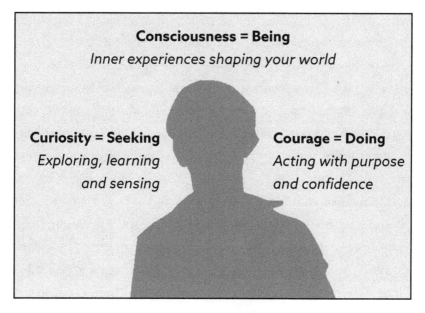

Consciousness = Being
Inner experiences shaping your world

Curiosity = Seeking
*Exploring, learning
and sensing*

Courage = Doing
*Acting with purpose
and confidence*

A reflection on the inner experiences shaping your character.

Consciousness (definition by Oxford Dictionary)
consciousness
noun

1. the state of being able to use your senses and mental powers to understand what is happening
2. the state of being aware of something
3. the ideas and opinions of a person or group

Enhancing leadership may sound abstract, but it's all about under-standing yourself better. Quick guidebooks on leadership often fall short when real-life events trigger human defensive mechanisms. The mental load of managing the complexity of organizational systems can become overwhelming. Today's leaders recognize their cognitive, physical, and emotional limitations and work on managing stress with character and grace. Consciousness is a process of integrating emo-tional, spiritual, cognitive, and physical aspects of life and the events that impact an individual's development in a social context.

Consciousness is a relatively new concept in Leadership Develop-ment, but it is the foundation of a holistic approach to leading in life and work. Being a leader means understanding who you are, your sur-roundings, and making sense of complex situations. Emotional con-nection to your personal history and experiences helps you respond with empathy and cognitive mastery. Consciousness involves aware-ness, attention, and mindful exploration of your emotions, without attaching judgment, shame, or guilt to life events. It is essential that you don't blame yourself for events that were perpetrated by others. Accepting your personal history is key to becoming a great leader. Being a leader is to recognize reality as is, beyond binary thinking.

Becoming a leader today is like a rollercoaster ride, full of antici-pation, unexpected curves and drops, and moments of fear and excite-ment. Although leading oneself is a bit more manageable, when you accept the challenge of leading other people and organizations, leader-ship can be quite complex. It involves connecting dots, making sense of data, and making confident decisions for strategic plans. But before discussing leadership in business, I will focus on leadership skills for yourself. Your journey starts when you enter the workforce, sharing goals and accountabilities with others. This phase can be both exciting and daunting, but it's a valuable learning experience. In your first five years at work, you'll discover your strengths, weaknesses, and emotional triggers that can make working in organizations challenging.

In my experience of working with leaders, I found that leadership skills are not solely acquired through training or traditional lectures. The most effective ways to gain new skills are the simplest yet challenging: having a clear mind and letting go of control. These are habits you can instill in yourself to foster a learning mindset. As a mental health provider, executive coach, trainer, and leadership development expert, I have experimented with many approaches in helping others discover their potential and build leadership skills. While there's no one-size-fits-all approach, everyone has the potential to tap into their own power and make a positive impact on the world. To gain access to that power, you will need to navigate your personal journey at your own pace, addressing any difficulties in your family, social or professional relationships. Just believe that it's worth the effort and time invested to discover your true aspirations, beliefs, and mission in life.

You might be asking why is there so much focus on knowing yourself when it is easier to just focus on what needs to be done? Yes, it's true that you can rationalize anything, create narratives to explain people's actions and justify your own based on performance goals. The problem is that relying solely on intellect can hinder your growth. Sometimes, the best way to cope with a difficult situation is to be a humble observer, learning from others and showing compassion. It is hard to empathize with someone else's reaction and still be able to accept your own feelings without being overwhelmed. Stay present, acknowledge your emotions, and slow down when facing new or difficult situations. Remember, what you used in the past may not apply to future experiences, and that's perfectly okay.

You might want to begin by examining your reactions starting with simple ones and moving to more complex ones. This can help you become aware of how your beliefs have been shaped by projecting your emotions onto events and groups. As an individual contributor who has struggled to express ideas during team meetings, you might have experienced situations where others seem to voice your thoughts before you do. This might trigger frustration by your ideas getting "stolen." However, instead of jumping to conclusions and judging others, try to pause and explore why it is difficult for you to verbalize your thoughts in group settings. Sometimes your underlying personal challenges and feelings of shame might be at play. Taking a moment to reflect without projecting your emotions onto others, can lead to personal growth. And this may lead you to explore your fears and their origins, ultimately helping you become more successful at what you want to achieve. Blaming others for your problems without self-reflection is a common mistake. It will be more rewarding for you to choose reflection over projection, and to analyze and not criticize.

Work as a team for collective success.

Teamwork is an amazing experience when all team members are conscious of the context, the diversity within the team, and the opportunity to create something that's greater than any individual's ideas. How you approach team discussions and collaborations will determine the quality of your teamwork and how others perceive you. It is important to learn to balance your authenticity with how you express yourself, so you feel comfortable with who you are while acting as part of a group. Show respect to others, embrace shared leadership, and you'll create a safe space for everyone to contribute and feel valued. This fosters psychological safety, allowing the team to experiment, learn from failures, and build a sense of belonging. It may sound easy, but it's important for everyone to be mindful of their words and actions to maintain positive interpersonal dynamics.

Consciousness is a state of being fully present in the moment, distinguishing between your past experiences and the reality you're witnessing right now. To be a conscious leader, you need to listen to others without letting your own thoughts interfere. Next on our journey, we'll dive into the power of curiosity—actively learning from others' opinions and perspectives. Maintaining a relentless focus on consciousness will boost self-awareness so you can sense the energy you generate as a leader. Consciousness is about "being" and living at a higher frequency, connecting the dots between people, their interactions, and sharing a purpose with intention. Consciousness in this context is the ability to use your inner strength to objectively assess challenges with optimism of a leader who believes in their ability to manage work-life dilemmas.

Your life is a mosaic of events within any given context, at each stage of your development, the impact may range from extremely harmful to extremely helpful. You are the only person who can make sense of memories in a way that serves you. A good exercise to help you see patterns of your behaviors is to make a list of the most memorable events in your life, in chronological order. This will help you identify root causes for some of your habits and how you react.

The development of a conscious mind requires attention to your health: physical, social, emotional, and spiritual. Consciousness is not a topic to be studied in isolation. Compartmentalizing your thoughts, memories, and views may provide temporary relief or a false sense of certainty. The world of work is clearly defined by ambiguity, uncertainty, and bias. And this is one of the dilemmas we face when becoming a leader in an organization. Acting with integrity, fully aligned with one's values while keeping stakeholders happy is often one of the greatest challenges. And yet, true leaders have mastered the ability to influence others while staying within their values and beliefs. Assessing and navigating the preferences of senior leaders in management teams requires patience and respect of diverse viewpoints. It's about finding the best solutions while honoring the perspectives of others.

Try to see an organization as a complex, adaptive, and dynamic organism. Beyond internal inconsistencies, you will also learn that customers, suppliers, partners, and other external entities have an impact on the workplace, the businesses, and its employees. That's why becoming a conscious leader who is discerning, self-aware, emotionally connected, curious, and courageous will prepare you for the new leadership consciousness that's emerging in business. Sharing power is already a practice among leaders who know organizations will only benefit from the collective commitment of its members. The concept of transparency in leadership is a major shift from management models of the past and has been shaping new work environments where information flows across the enterprise without friction.

Even if you have not been in a traditional position of leadership, chances are you've faced situations in your personal life, school, or work where you felt a sense of agency and responsibility. Think about the three main leadership qualities: Consciousness, Curiosity, and Courage, and recall a time when you applied all three elements to understand, resolve, or manage a situation successfully. This exercise helps you put in perspective the hard work involved in staying true to yourself while listening, understanding consequences, and taking a less popular stance within your community. Consciousness evolves by being open to the world's signals, making sense of information, staying present in the moment to act effectively. Leadership is an art best experienced, not learned in the classroom where the controlled environments make responses seem easier. Bridging the gap between a simulated exercise and real-life events is a crucial step in your development. To strike a better balance, stay centered, be present, and apply lessons learned from actual experiences.

Consciousness is the foundation of human wisdom, with potential to significantly improve our future. In a world marked by divisive binary thinking, it enables us to embrace diverse perspectives, consider contextual facts, and apply critical thinking to complex issues. The conscious mind values all resources, including feelings, emotional experiences, and cognition to foster unity amid imperfections. A conscious leader is selfless in their pursuit of positive outcomes for the collective well-being. They know that on a cloudy day, the sun is still shinning, and they lift themselves above the clouds to remain balanced, and flow through the moment knowing that everything is temporary.

Consciousness means staying present without getting lost in thoughts or reactions. As a conscious leader, your role is to be present, understand your environment, and still be able to act effectively. The collective consciousness is shifting as people are becoming more aware of the impact we have on the planet, on each other, and how our anger, hatred, and negative emotions are harming our own well-being. The business consciousness is also shifting as we are now confronted with new realities, new workforce demands. Leading today requires awareness of how our actions impact others and the world.

Companies are now under scrutiny by a wider range of stakeholders, shareholders, and customers who are weighing the impact of greed and irresponsible actions on the environment. Environmental, Social, and Corporate Governance (ESG) are pressuring boards of directors to be more accountable for corporate actions. At the same time, organizations are struggling to find and retain the best talent with the right skills. The workforce is becoming more influential, and it is challenging traditional leadership. Innovative companies are responding by transforming the workplace, promoting inclusion, and sharing power across functions to create a new way of organizing.

The past no longer is, the future is not yet here; there is only one moment in which life is available, and that is the present moment. – Thich Nhat Hanh

CHAPTER 6

Leadership Expression: Curiosity = Seeking

There is a competitive advantage when leaders are learners.

Your success depends on your ability to connect, co-create, and contribute in an evolving workplace that values innovation and collaboration. And this is an exceptional challenge if you were accustomed to limiting yourself to a prescribed role and position with clear job descriptions and individual performance, evaluated at the end of the year. The way work is done is changing quickly and the core capability in team effectiveness and inclusion is your curiosity. Adapting to shifting environments and strategies that are dynamic, helping members of the ecosystem explore new thinking, and partnering for the discovery of new operating systems, leaders are taking actions that matter in a sustainable manner. Navigating the contradictions of an everchanging world with integrity, and understanding the shift from problems to dilemmas, tensions, and conflicts, will better equip you to respond to unexpected situations and events. As opposed to problems that must be resolved through a fixed solution, dilemmas are usually at the intersection of dual realities that must be considered carefully before you can act in the workplace successfully. You are rarely dealing with absolute realities at work. Being curious allows for multiple inputs and creates an openness to receiving information from a diverse group of people. Curiosity is essential in your search for new thinking and fresh ideas.

When IBM's Institute for Business Value (IBV) asked CEOs in 2010 about the most critical skills for the future, they ranked creativity as the #1 skill for senior leaders. It's been a long time since the study's publication, and there is no evidence of CEOs focusing their energy on becoming more creative, since most organizations have been dealing with digital transformations and continuous disruptions in their industries. I believe it is a vital human capability that drives learning and innovation. In this process, leaders need to be open to letting go of preconceived notions and be willing to experiment, paving a way to the new style of leadership that promotes growth in their organizations. While data and reports offer insights, they have their limitations. Leaders who share power and co-create with their clients and employees recognize the need for divergent thinking to enhance their strategies. Relying solely on data can lead to analysis paralysis, but combining intuition, knowledge, curiosity, risk taking, and context-specific experimentation allows for innovative approaches that stay ahead of the competition, as historical data can't provide a path to the future.

Companies copying best practices from competitors miss the chance to build a unique culture that takes them further in their industries. Benchmarking for so-called "best practices" becomes a safety net, offering proven success methods, but these practices are not tailored to their specific context and end up falling short. Today's leaders need to develop digital, data, and analytical skills while nurturing human qualities like consciousness, curiosity, and courage. Take what happened in 2021/2022 regarding the "return" to the office strategies of major corporations. Thousands of surveys and studies asked professionals about their preferences, but most leaders, unable to truly understand their employees' individual needs, turned to consulting firms and peer companies for advice. Despite the lack of experience, most CEOs opted to follow "best practices" and asked their employees to return to the office two or three days a week. The trend took off, but it led to the "the great resignation," as many executives applied past experiences to a new dilemma without engaging their teams in co-creating the new workplace.

Seeing new contexts through old lenses will not help you manage new challenges. You could call this transition a great experiment that revealed the lack of innovation and curiosity among today's organizational leaders. Before 2019, most CEOs and their senior teams would laugh at anyone suggesting that remote work could increase productivity. They've been conditioned by traditional business school thinking and peer pressure to stick to the prescribed frameworks. These unwritten rules and the behavioral habits in hierarchical companies cultivate complacency and may lack the ingredients of future-ready workplaces. The key to this new leadership in progressive organizations is the willingness to embrace curiosity, crowdsourcing, and co-creation to find new ways of working and conducting business.

To avoid outdated leadership, examine your beliefs about idea generation and decision making in your circle. Many studies suggest leaders overestimate their intellect and worth. In today's fast-paced organizations, ecosystems evolve rapidly. Members connect, converse, and solve problems through conversation. Senior leaders must balance stakeholders' expectations and adapt to changing tensions in their businesses. Empathizing with leaders who succeeded in stable conditions within their industries will help you understand how difficult it is to change one's mindset, behavior, and habits. To be influential, understand how to influence leaders who prioritize operational efficiency, despite it not being a growth-oriented approach in the global economy.

To drive innovation, executives need diverse perspectives, humility, and emotional control. Effective leaders value feedback, respond thoughtfully, and create a safe environment. Great leadership is learned and practiced through self-improvement and curiosity. To inspire innovation in teams, consider innovation labs that encourage idea-sharing and use Design Thinking tools for collaborative problem-solving.

Feedback is an essential skill and demands curiosity to learn about your own triggers. Sheila Heen and Doug Stone in their book *Thanks for the Feedback*, write about the three triggers you may experience. The first is the "truth trigger," where you immediately reject the feedback without considering its value. The second is the "relationship trigger," questioning the feedback giver's authority. Lastly, the "self-identity trigger" involves feeling threatened when feedback challenges your self-identity. To receive feedback effectively, stay open-minded, assess the information, and decide how to use it through curiosity, reflection, and acceptance.

Every piece of feedback has value when approached with a learning mindset. Saying "no" to some feedback doesn't mean you're insincere when accepting others. You must be open to learning and sometimes you may just say "thank you for the feedback." People offer feedback to help you improve or to support you as a team leader. Or perhaps, in resistance to a new idea. Regardless of the motivations, every interaction will help you navigate change resistance more effectively.

Be engaged, not attached.

The goal is to be fully engaged in what you do in life and at work, but be mindful of emotional attachments to ideas, people, and projects. They can hinder objectivity and limit opportunities for curious exploration. Sometimes, you get deeply involved in projects, solely focused on executing your ideas, missing out on diverse thinking that could enhance innovation. That's why most future-ready organizations embrace Design Thinking which allows teams to co-create. Great leaders empower purpose-driven teams with diverse skills and growth mindset, all aligned to a common mission.

Allowing for collective intelligence to grow, you create learning experiences away from self-centered ideas. It's not easy to stop being competitive and always trying to be right. Like everyone, you will face anxieties about your capabilities, stress from unrealistic demands, and resistance to rigid directions. The key is to ignite your team's passion by working on the problem or project together. Remember, you are stronger as a diverse, creative team, and great leaders empower their followers, creating an environment free from fear and shame.

Developing communications skills like diplomacy and tact is critical in organizational life and it complements your curiosity. At times, you will need to use tact to navigate conflict or address complex situations involving multiple opinions and interests. It's important to let go of your own perspective and listen curiously to others. For instance, when discussing diversity, equity, and inclusion, different group leaders may have various concerns. These situations offer valuable opportunities to learn from each other and create a shared strategic purpose. But to achieve a collective commitment to Diversity, Equity, Inclusion and Belonging (DEI&B), leaders must elevate their thinking, and act with tact and respect for each group's point of view, driven by curiosity.

At this point you might be thinking that becoming a great leader is an exhausting endeavor, but please remind yourself that your mental, cognitive, and emotional systems are adaptive, and will evolve with your commitment to self-awareness, self-acceptance, and self-actualization. You are a complex human being with the power to survive difficult events. You can control your reactions through curiosity, reflection, expression, integration, and support. At times, you will need to seek professional help to get you through trauma, and I hope you know there's no shame in that. I personally experienced the healing power of mental health services after spending a few years in the United States. Childhood traumas, environmental anxiety, being an immigrant, and starting my adult life from a vulnerable place accumulated in general anxiety, sometimes as panic attacks. Seeking help was the way to a better life and a successful career in the new country.

Psychotherapy was transformational during a very tough time in my life. It took courage to accept it, to share it, and to let go of the shame associated with it. In addition to my own struggles, it became clear that the AIDS/HIV crisis and the loss of two good friends in Brazil, were impacting me greatly. Today, I live a happy life filled with optimism and the inner strength to face challenges with confidence. I hope that as you read these pages, you'll learn that being confident, successful, and valued are not exclusive privileges. The real challenge is to be curious about your own story, life events, and emotions, and to overcome the fear that shields you from pain. Embrace your whole self with authenticity, even though the journey of self-awareness and healing isn't easy. The most admired leaders show vulnerability, focus on the collective purpose, and connect with others. They acknowledge negative emotions, self-doubt, and fear but handle them adaptively, moving forward with the belief that they're doing their best to be true to themselves and achieve acceptance of their life history, a significant accomplishment in a fulfilling life.

Let's talk about being assessed as a leader in an organization. To support your career progression, most mentors and senior leaders will assess your maturity in dealing with ambiguity, uncertainty, and adverse events that require emotional intelligence and critical thinking. Mentors are looking for a leader who can set aside their own needs in service of others. But the question is how does one acquire this leadership maturity? Well, showing interest in those around you and engaging with them is a good start. When you join a healthy workplace, you become a part of a community where members are accountable for each other. The future of work is about creating a vibrant diverse community of radical collaborators who are much more powerful together than any single individual. Leadership will be shared among all employees as they take on the responsibility for decisions and outcomes. In the less hierarchical organization, you will experience distributed power for distributed teams. To be fully effective in your role as a team player, you must adopt a style of leadership that's oriented toward the collective. This is the goal of your self-awareness, social and cultural intelligence, as well as critical thinking, analytics, and communicational development. As a leader you will be challenged to stay authentic with your employees, and for that to happen, you must believe in the power of shared experiences and the positive impact you can make by expressing your unique voice at work, while respecting yourself and others equally.

The emergence of a new kind of leadership seems to be the natural progression in re-engaging the workforce after the chaos we have been experiencing in the first quarter of this century. While many companies have crafted an image of progressiveness and empathy by prominently featuring words like diversity and innovation to attract talent on their websites, this communication tactic has lost the desired impact. The reality is that most organizations continue to cling to unhealthy business practices. Decisions are made at the top with low commitment from senior leaders and their teams to change the way employees experience work. If we could focus on the employee experience as much as we focus on the customer experience, organizations would see enhanced performance by using respect for autonomy and a belief in the skills and abilities of all people. To create a thriving new workplace, we must explore fresh organizational and work designs with curiosity and the courage to discard old norms and charts, a topic we'll delve into further in the next section on Courage in organizational leaders.

Leadership serves as the driving force for teams who share purpose and goals. This is particularly important during transformations and growth periods in an organization with multiple business lines and functions that tend to resist enterprise changes. Collective leadership aligns strategies, fosters commitment to transformational goals and enhances employee performance. The reality is that some businesses will ultimately decline while others will grow, and that's a dilemma for most executives in charge of a turnaround. Like an organism, organizations need each employee to play their role in creating a culture in which there is a strategic understanding of the company's direction, and everyone contributes to the desired outcomes. In the twenty-first century, this complex perspective can provide a competitive edge, combining data, insights, and full engagement, all driven by curiosity as the catalyst for transformation.

Being curious is like exploring the world as a child, with neither hidden agendas nor preconceived ideas about what's to be discovered. As a leader, you should nurture your ability to be surprised by new information and perspectives, making others feel valued and heard, and creating psychological safety. Most employees seek to understand what's permitted to happen and allowed to be done in a workspace. Future-ready organizations are letting go of old programs and policies in favor of open dialogue and engagement systems that can develop a culture of experimentation, teamwork, and most importantly, authentic diversity of thought. In these environments, discussions are candid, diverse opinions are welcomed without hostility, and people feel a sense of belonging, leading to commitment and going the extra mile to help each other succeed.

CHAPTER 7

Leadership Expression: Courage = Doing

Act with purpose and confidence.

It may sound scary to think about courage in the workplace, given hierarchical dynamics and individual performance evaluations. But it is also liberating to learn that you can cultivate courage as an asset for your professional and personal growth. In this discussion, I'll explore how you can discern when and how to apply courage in your career. At a meeting I was facilitating with senior leaders and high-potential individuals, one of the employees asked a senior executive: "How much authority do you really have to make big decisions?" Without hesitation, the leader smiled and replied: "I have as much authority as my courage allows me to have." This succinctly illustrates how personal empowerment stems from individual conviction and confidence to act with resolve. Leadership is energy that requires self-awareness, self-acceptance, and values-based behaviors that manifest core beliefs and ethical alignment to the organization's strategy and operating system. Believing in your courage as energy that creates value is an essential approach to acting when the stakes are high.

Courage is a vital skill that empowers you to take action, express your ideas, and set a positive example in your environment. It thrives in environments that provide psychological safety. Research shows that people need to feel comfortable expressing their ideas without fear of backlash. Courage starts with seeing yourself for who you truly are and being able to grow from many experiences. Being able to own your prejudices, biases, as well as creativity and innovative thinking, you can set yourself on a trajectory of continuous learning, allowing the self to be influenced by new information. Courage to be yourself, to deviate from group thinking in a team meeting are behaviors that build confidence. In today's agile organizations, it is not uncommon for teams to course-correct, learn from failures, and move forward, learning from their successes and errors. This shift requires support and encouragement from senior leaders to promote courage as a cultural norm, so employees can achieve their goals.

Clarity creates capacity.

It may sound simple, but there is a great deal of courage at play in creating clarity in business. Employees often grapple with uncertainty about the company's direction, leading to stress and uncertainty about their own roles. The courage to change how things have been done, to empower distributed teams, and provide clear direction across departments is essential for a positive impact on the organization. When employees lack a shared understanding of the workplace changes, they become disengaged. Leaders must have the courage to communicate transparently to build trust with their employees. They should consolidate ideas into coherent messages that make employees feel included in the evolving strategy, adapting to internal and external events. Acknowledging imperfection and being honest with those seeking clarity helps leaders manage ambiguity in the workplace. This involves using adaptive coping skills when life gets overwhelming, and by allowing themselves to be vulnerable over being perfect.

Learn to recognize patterns and insights.

Success is an ever-changing journey, filled with unexpected twists and valuable lessons. Embrace detours and setbacks as opportunities for growth. Resilience and courage are companions on this road, helping you navigate and steer your career in the right direction. Observe your surroundings, feel the impact of others, and consider various options as you move forward. Reflecting on past experiences and identifying behavior patterns can guide your next steps. Don't limit yourself to a single goal; sometimes, the best opportunities arise unexpectedly. That's when you can reflect, question advice, and make your own decisions aligned with your success and happiness. Courage arises from assessing situations, acknowledging fears, and having confidence in your actions, even if they cause tension. It's a blend of self-assuredness and awareness of consequences.

The ability to recognize patterns is a great life skill, especially when tackling complex business challenges. It helps you understand where leaders are taking a company and how customers make decisions. Try experimenting by observing people around you, connecting the dots, building hypothesis, and deciphering hidden messages in behavior patterns. At the end of the day, our behavior patterns shield our secrets, fueled by shame, guilt, or embarrassment. To lead a healthy life, it's essential to notice these patterns and be willing to change them. It takes courage—the courage to confront fears, achieve self-acceptance, and act. Great leaders act with certainty after thorough research and analysis. Courage means being aware of potential outcomes as well as risks and still taking action with confidence.

Howard Gardner, in his book *Five Minds for the Future*, talks about the importance of the Synthesizing Mind. It's crucial for understanding and making sense of the information and data, in our environment.

Leaders need to cultivate the ability to gather information from diverse sources into coherent strategies. While technology and AI can help recognize patterns in customer and employee behavior, data privacy concerns and regulations are important. Pattern recognition is a valuable process for innovation, allowing you to explore various data and ideas before shaping them into actionable goals. This can be truly learned only if you're able to expand your network to include diverse perspectives, even if they challenge your existing ideas. Having the courage to let go of the need to be right is a sign that you are becoming a mature leader.

Using data and gaining insights is how most of us learn to recognize patterns. However, data by itself isn't enough to make sense of others and the world. Datasets must be carefully selected as we often choose them to confirm our beliefs, which can lead to inaccurate conclusions. I've seen some attribute employee turnover to low performers leaving the company to avoid performance improvement actions. But analyzing exit interviews and engagement reports revealed that poor management was the main driver of attrition. Data and analytics can provide insights into behaviors of those leaving the organization, but you must collect and analyze this data before inferring the root causes of dynamics like attrition. Avoid adjusting reality to evade accountability, as this is not the behavior of a responsible leader.

Organizational Network Analysis (ONA) is your organizational compass.

In today's workplaces, we're going beyond traditional charts and structures to understand how value is created. Experts in Organizational Network Analysis (ONA), assert that by studying how people communicate and collaborate, we can uncover the secrets of success in modern organizations. ONA is a valuable skill to have in the new world of work. It involves looking beyond your immediate team or department and seeing the organization as a network of experts collaborating across various teams. Additionally, the traditional senior leaders in the hierarchy may not be the influencers of the organization's culture. ONA allows you to identify hidden figures and map the real influencers across the networked organization.

ONA looks at interactions, frequency of contact, and quality of these relationships to identify key individuals, the "de facto" leaders, who drive success. Known as "Cultural Catalysts" these leaders are found in a variety of roles and levels in the organization. ONA enhances processes, speeds decision-making, and improves collaboration by pinpointing knowledge holders regardless of their role. It's vital for a positive culture, revealing influencers and informal leaders who act on their principles. Understanding social capital as a professional currency is a required skill for career advancement. As future-ready companies interconnect, ONA and Talent Supply Management gain importance.

Be comfortable not being perfect.

Courageous gestures of kindness are important in the development of great leadership. We've all made unfair judgments, felt guilt, and shame. Acknowledging this and realizing we can negatively affect others is the first step in developing emotional intelligence. These difficult insights help you respond with authenticity and transparency, recognizing your emotions and fears. The final step is self-acceptance, embracing imperfections without losing self-esteem. Being conscious of your impact allows you to change for the better.

I learned a beautiful lesson from the head of a global business when I was organizing a meeting in Singapore for one thousand senior executives. The event would start with a panel of leaders from client companies who were preparing to tell us their honest opinions about our services and how we could improve them. Three days before the start of the event, I had to find the courage to call the executive sponsor to let him know that all three clients had backed out of the panel. Our team braced for the frustrated reaction that has become so common in corporate settings, but instead, he calmly responded: "Thank you for letting me know. Things happen . . . Can we find other clients?" It was an amazing positive response that boosted our commitment to finding new panelists. By the next morning we had four new clients who accepted the invitation to participate. Leaders' attitudes toward their team directly impacts how motivated employees are in their work.

You're learning these leadership skills to access your subconscious motivations, break free from learned helplessness, and recognize deeply rooted beliefs that may be holding you back. It's a challenging process, but it leads to a unique life that's designed by you. Having the courage to change careers, or pursue your passions, even if loved ones disagree, can be amazing achievements. Families evolve, and culture is constantly changing for the better.

Optimistic leaders see the future as a better version of the present and are empowered to make a positive impact on the world. Facing criticism and self-discovery can be confusing, but focusing on your truths can be very helpful. Remember, personal growth is a long journey, and you're in control. Being a leader is altruistic and deserves respect. Honesty, tough conversations, and trust-building shape your character and self-identity. No one can tell you how to live your life, and taking accountability for your own development is a step toward happiness and peace. Stay centered and aware of others while finding your own path.

CHAPTER 8

The Power of Human-Centered Leadership

Lead with empathy and compassion.

Empathy is a vital skill for human-centric leaders of the future. It's crucial for building strong cultures, effective teams, and irresistible workplaces. However, in a fast-paced world, it can be challenging. Leaders often face quick problem-solving, dilemmas, and the pressure to support others dealing with burnout. Burnout is widespread, leaving many emotionally drained and overwhelmed. To truly empathize, you need emotional well-being, which can be tough when you're exhausted and struggling to focus on others.

Today, beyond the usual workplace pressures, people are rethinking the importance of money-driven goals. They're searching for purpose and significance in their jobs, wanting to feel that what they do matters. This shift may be influenced by recent events like the 2008 financial crisis, and the COVID-19 pandemic, which exposed the vulnerability of our health, financial systems, and job security. These disruptions shifted our perceptions of reality in the workplace and the fallacy of long-term job security. One of the unexpected outcomes of these changes is the remote work revolution which became the catalyst for a new collective consciousness across the global workforce. Employee expectations of more purposeful and meaningful work are at the core of a human-centered leadership mindset, which is fundamentally fueled by emotional attunement and empathy.

Compassion is also a deeper emotional connection that drives human-centered decisions and culture. Empathy means understanding someone's perspective without being judgmental. Becoming a compassionate leader, however, involves actively addressing group suffering, social injustices, or global conflicts impacting vulnerable populations. Being compassionate might be one of the most rewarding experiences for those interested in enhancing interpersonal relationships. Compassion means sharing others' emotional experiences and offering support during tough times. In a leadership role, compassion can lead to solutions that minimize the impact of decisions, like offering training for employees affected by changes, to help them find new opportunities. Compassionate leaders are vocal about others' needs and actively seek solutions for challenging situations.

Being compassionate towards yourself is a positive step in managing emotions and learning from experiences, even when there's no instant gratification or reward. It's hard to help others if you're out of touch with your own emotions. You can start by journaling about personal events, especially those negatively impacting your self-perception. This helps you learn and reframe how you handle tough emotions in the future. Being compassionate can help you avoid unhealthy coping behaviors, driven by guilt or shame. It's common to blame yourself to protect loved ones. Developing compassion for yourself, along with consciousness, curiosity, and courage, allows you to address suppressed feelings and build better coping skills. This prepares you to empathize with others' experiences more clearly. Once you learn to observe and accept your own emotions, empathy and compassion will help you cope with whatever comes at you. It's important to know how to stay in the moment, seek support, and avoid isolation or depression, especially when facing situations that seem overwhelming and helpless, possibly leading to burnout.

You have by now noticed that the integration of your professional and personal life is inevitable when you are a human-centered leader. Business and society are becoming intrinsically connected through purpose and humanity. In the new world of work, organizations will be mostly open systems interacting with a wide range of social groups, institutions, and communities built with diversity in mind: including people of color, non-binary talent, neuro-diverse, and underserved individuals. Our interconnected social systems are becoming more transparent and accessible worldwide. Traditional boundaries that hid corporate interests are fading, leading executives to consider the impact of their actions on people and the planet. Environmental, Social, and Governance (ESG) practices reflect this shift toward human-centered leadership. Companies embracing these strategies will attract talent and build positive brands. However, leaders driven solely by ambition may prioritize profit over everything else. While they may gain some traction initially, followers will likely shift toward leaders who support their growth and career success.

Share your leadership experience with your team.

As I have mentioned before, leaders share power to achieve common goals. As a team member, you can demonstrate your character, ability, and collaboration skills to build the trust necessary for your team to achieve the best outcomes. Effective teams thrive on trust, and it's crucial that team members approach interactions with positive intent, share their ideas and feedback, and respect differing opinions. Being open to influence, and influencing others, allows diverse ideas to come together for collective missions. While team members don't always have to agree, they must commit to a shared direction, engage in ongoing dialogue, and establish transparent communication norms to work effectively. In essence, you can disagree with others on the team, but you will need to support the team's collective decision.

Building trust is all about discovery. Actively listening to others helps you explore new perspectives on problems and opportunities, a crucial skill for adaptability. The professional of the future must be adaptable to the pace of change that has become the norm in most workplaces. You may be working on one thing today, then receive different guidance the next, as new insights lead to new goals. A nimble, adaptable, and cohesive team can adjust its contributions to fit the context, making trust a vital part of the change process. Trust involves believing in your team members, sharing concerns and fears, and finding common ground to foster a sense of belonging. When you lead with an open mind and heart, you'll experience a more fulfilling work life. Cultivating a positive intent is essential when joining a new team, as it paves the way for effective communication, collective understanding, and minimizes conflicts arising from individual interests that hinder group success.

As you step into the modern career mindset, you'll realize your resilience, ability to handle workplace challenges, and adaptability are stronger than you thought. Facing difficulties and conflicts at work helps you develop skills to deal with similar situations in the future. See the world for what it is and find new ways to shape it and navigate it with fluidity. Living on the edge of the future is better than being dragged backward or stuck in the mud of the past. Take a moment to think about tough situations at work or in life and spot the behavior patterns you tend to show in similar contexts. Personally, I've realized that one of my triggers relates to fairness and justice. In the past, I faced false accusations and the frustration of not being able to prove the truth triggered quick emotional reactions when I sensed a risk of being wrongly accused again. Without reflection and self-control, I saw many situations as threats because of the fear from past events. This self-referencing process interfered with my ability to listen without reacting defensively. When fear took over, everything seemed like a danger signal, leading to impulsive actions and misunderstandings. Recognizing these flaws wasn't easy, but it's part of personal growth. I'm proud of uncovering these traits, which will help me stay present and become a better leader.

You must center yourself.

Reflecting on your impulses can greatly improve your relationships and bring out your best self. The habit of reflection is key to understanding your conflicts with those around you. If you see yourself always arguing for your position as the "right" one, then I would suggest you apply empathy and see the situation from their perspective. Empathy is a Power Skill you can't neglect as you build your professional reputation and develop your leadership skills. Being an empathic professional allows others to express their emotions, especially about difficult subjects, and share their fears, knowing that you'll try to understand them without criticism. You might want to say something like, "I'd like to understand your point of view so I can learn why this is important to you." To be effective as an empathic leader, you will need to set your needs aside; know your own feelings, avoid denial, accept the fear, and the impulse to fix other people's problems. Instead, focus on attentive listening with an open heart and a curious mindset. A quiet mind is an excellent tool for truly understanding others' realities. And paradoxically, you must be at peace with yourself to be present for others.

As you advance in your career, you will encounter colleagues who may rely on you for support, and it's how you engage with them and set your boundaries that will help you be there for them. In social work school, I learned very early to "start where the client is," which means knowing that we can't push people to point C if they are still on point A and still need to move through B first. So, when you become frustrated with people who are not where you want them to be, it's likely because you are expecting them to step out of their comfort zone prematurely. Instead, work on helping them consider the next step and give them space to decide and act when they feel ready. This approach applies to yourself too. Sometimes, you may get frustrated for not being ahead in life, at work, or school. Remind yourself that a measure of success is not based on comparisons or titles. You are where you need to be. However, this doesn't exempt you from the responsibility of striving for high performance and having tough conversations when necessary.

The second lesson I learned in social work is to avoid "rescuing" others from their problems or emotional distress. Instead, we can empathize, offer help, or suggest resources when they're ready. It's natural to want to ease someone's pain, but we all go through tough times. Our role is to meet their needs, sometimes simply by being there, without rushing to solve everything. Witness and listen; don't always try to rescue. The workplace mirrors the larger world; balancing your experiences with empathy is crucial.

As you've likely experienced in your career, having complete control over all aspects of your life is just unrealistic. The future will bring rapid changes at work, including new structures, teams, and strategies. Adaptability is key in this ever-evolving landscape. It means embracing change, even when it's not linear, and being self-aware about your attachment to the past. Changes will not ask permission to enter your life, but how you turn them into opportunities will determine your success.

Being in touch with what's happening in your industry is a must, and you will need to take all the data available and synthesize it to make sense of the information to form your own opinions. While many experts discuss the future, predicting outcomes isn't foolproof. Knowing your competitors, emerging technologies, and the major factors impacting the economy is enough for you to start adapting to a new way of assessing your business.

Assess your own path against what successful people did to reach the top, with a mindful and balanced view. What you see online isn't always the whole truth, especially for C-suite roles. Take a moment to understand what really matters to you as a unique individual with talent, skills, and emotional needs. Instead of a fixed destination, set a direction for your career, using your own compass. Sometimes the path is clear, other times it's unclear. Regardless, let your ambition be guided by your beliefs and values. Create a personal brand that reflects the human-centered leader you want to be, with a voice that echoes your positive beliefs. As a leader, one of the toughest tasks is figuring out the best way forward.

Leading oneself is fulfilling when you accept every day as an open door and see others not as competitors but as contributors to your collective success. As you assess your life experiences, learn to leverage your coping skills in face of changes and challenges, remember that you can always refer to past experiences to help you find new solutions for the present. Allow for others to support you and help you along the way. Find a mentor, a friend, or even a stranger to share their journey with you. The future isn't solely shaped by your dreams, it's influenced by your interactions with the world. Find what motivates you at each stage of your professional growth, and follow the signals from your heart, even if your interests lead you on various paths. Harness positive energy and channel it toward achieving your leadership goals and taking action.

Communicate from the heart.

We've talked about the three Leadership Expressions (Consciousness, Curiosity, and Courage) and a few skills to help you navigate the complexity of life at work. Communication is a cornerstone skill that encompasses various aspects of your work life. Effective communication involves managing your physical reactions, expressions, body language, tone, and intent. Reflecting on your communication style and its origins is a valuable exercise. Personally, I grew up in a noisy environment where needing to shout was common to be heard. I often chose silence, enabling me to truly understand what people meant. This quiet observation made me more introspective, and as an introvert, I honed my ability to navigate new situations through observation. It wasn't until college that I found my voice and realized my potential for setting goals and developing new capabilities. Rather than dwelling on missed opportunities for self-expression, I cherished my skills of observation, listening, and reflection as tools to navigate the world.

You are shaped by your stories, preferences, and inherent traits, but your brain is malleable, and your personal growth journey allows you to develop your identity and voice. This is incredibly valuable in your search for a career or a place in the world. No matter where you come from, you have the power to decide where to go. As an immigrant from Brazil, I often blamed my poor education and lack of opportunities for not being able to move quicker in my assimilation to American life. Learning English was also a years-long effort. Limited language skills kept me working in restaurants for a long time. Expressing myself didn't come easily, and the frustration of being a college graduate working as a busboy taught me some very valuable life lessons. Experiencing undervaluation and social invisibility due to societal norms gives you empathy for others' struggles. I take pride in my journey, as it shaped me, despite its frustrations, emotional toll, and isolation.

You have a past, but it is important to stay in the moment and appreciate the here and now before looking back. There is no need to wait for a future event to celebrate who you have become and how your life adds value to many others. Just being yourself, connected to the energy that surrounds you, is enough to explore the complexity of life. Becoming successful is a continuous effort that entails the development of skills and new perspective on situations and people. Allowing yourself to be selfless gives you an opportunity to see others with compassion. As a leader, create the habit of continuous learning and thriving amid challenges and new experiences. Remember that blocking your emotions and rationalizing your fixed mindset will not help you grow as a person, even if it takes you to better paying jobs. The path to wealth and prestige, without experiencing your life fully, is not worth the trip. You can aim to make a good living and support your dreams, but don't forget to listen to what others are offering you on the way there. Practice gratitude for what you've achieved while staying present to savor life as it happens. Gratitude is a positive force that lifts your spirit and empowers your authentic leadership.

CHAPTER 9

Teams are the New Unit of Value

Why, what, how, when, where, and with whom do we work?

I chose to write this book with minimal reliance on third-party data, studies, theories, and frameworks, as I believe the world of work is changing at the speed of thinking, and sharing my observations as a talent strategist, employee, leadership coach, and future of work enthusiast, gives me the opportunity to see ahead of the curve, avoiding the "Shiny Object Syndrome" (SOS). All the choices you and I make shape who we are. Sharing leadership and power with others is the best way to support the collective success. I hope you're now prepared to explore new ways of working, develop essential human skills for joyful collaboration, and doing so regardless of your chosen work environment, diversity dimensions, socio-economic background, appearance, or ideologies. Work is fundamentally about achieving positive outcomes as a team, even when working independently. This section of the book will guide you in building successful relationships and navigating organizational cultures that extend to the broader business ecosystem.

Teams come in different shapes and forms. Whether you're part of an intact team led by a manager all doing similar work, or working in cross-functional teams, or an independent professional working with an agile team, you will need social skills to connect to the team's purpose and meet the needs of your customers and clients. Regardless of the team setup, excelling in a social context requires using all your senses and skills, including cognitive and personal abilities, to contribute, collaborate, and deliver great work. In this chapter, we'll explore the attributes that will help you adapt to teams with diverse and inclusive cultures, and learn to identify the conditions that may hinder the team's progress.

Have essential conversations with your team.

Organizations are reimagining how they develop critical capabilities that set them apart in the market. Leaders are expanding their search for top talent through location-independent recruitment, often bringing in skills from temporary independent contractors. Forward-thinking companies are overhauling how work is done, leveraging technology, robotics, automation, Generative AI with Large Language Models (LLM), and machine learning. These tools are combined with the expertise of professionals from various talent pools.

We're witnessing the rise of independent professionals who work as fractional talent through engagement contracts and platforms. The open talent community is also offering services in unconventional employment arrangements. Traditional outsourcing is still in use, with partnerships formed with new service organizations. Workforces are being composed as an open system of skills and capabilities, allowing the formation of agile teams, innovation groups, and cross-functional working teams to advance strategies and goals exponentially.

To begin your journey in the evolving workplace, it's essential to recognize that your family was your first "team" in life. This wasn't a conscious choice, but it's where you learned to interact with others, understand their behaviors, and figure out how to achieve your goals. Your early experiences in the family system shaped your environment, influencing your responses and instincts for survival, growth, and self-sufficiency.

As you grew, you ventured beyond your caregivers' embrace, testing your individuality, and taking risks to become self-reliant within your limitations. Your upbringing, including interactions with siblings, parents, teachers, and your overall environment, greatly influenced your personality and behaviors. These experiences, both positive and negative, formed the foundation of your adult life, often unconsciously.

It's important to note that the skills that helped you navigate your early years may not be the most effective ones for success as a professional and leader in today's world.

Childhood is fragile. It demands empathic relationships from caretakers whose parenting skills will define how the child experiences the world. No parent is perfect, and by now you have shared multiple situations with others in the outside world, learning that life's unpleasant moments are inevitable. The great news is that you're resilient, able to manage pain, build strength, and enjoy exciting moments. You have experienced a wide range of emotions throughout life and have overcome many encounters with those who may or may not have had the capacity to build positive relationships with you. But no matter where you came from, you can think, reflect, regain control, seek help, and achieve closure. Furthermore, entering the workforce is not an opportunity to let go of the past, rather, it's an opportunity to learn, observe, and recognize what coping skills you have developed up until now and integrate your life experiences.

Entering the workforce, starting in a new school, a new hobby, or moving to a new town, are considered life transitions that will challenge your capacity to learn and adapt to new realities. The complicating factors in these experiences are your emotions, memories, and mindset. If you perceive changes as coming from others, it's hard to process them as positive. You may go through these experiences and somehow find ways of coping and adjusting, but not fully embrace them. Your ability to adapt to these changes defines how you react to other experiences as a professional. In a sense, the workplace is an experiment in socialization that you can use as an opportunity for healing old wounds, but knowing that you're guided by your own values, beliefs, love, and your potential to be your best.

Take a moment to think back to a significant change that happened in your life during your first ten years. What comes to mind? Did your family decide to move? Did your best friend move to another town? Were there disruptions in your immediate family? Whatever the events were, you likely remember the feelings that washed over you when you realized that things were shifting. Think about your thoughts, feelings, and reactions.

It's important to acknowledge and respect the emotions that surfaced during different phases of your life. Reflecting on these past events can provide insights into how you learned to cope and express your feelings when faced with challenges. You may discover that there were instances when you didn't have the opportunity to express or process these events in a way that helped you move forward. You can repeat this exercise several times to identify your typical response to events that are beyond your control. Whether it's anger, sadness, apathy, anxiety, or any other reaction, it may have been your way of dealing with the belief that you couldn't influence reality. However, during these moments of reflection, you have the chance to reframe the event, adjust your perspective, or simply observe your thoughts, allowing you to recall these memories with fewer emotional reactions.

As you step into the workforce, dive into teams, groups, and projects with an open mind. Embrace the opportunity to learn from your peers while contributing your best ideas. It's crucial to pick up techniques for building trust, fostering connections, and, most importantly, becoming an inclusive team member.

Let's kick things off by exploring pivotal moments that shape how your colleagues perceive you within an organization. Your first thirty days on the job, especially when you're entering a new team, company, or role with a new boss, are critical for forming impressions. When you start meeting your new coworkers, consider establishing a few rules of engagement that showcase your strengths right from the get-go. If you are an introvert who struggles when introduced in a group setting, you might want to set up individual meetings with your colleagues before a large team meeting. This will give you an opportunity to establish a rapport with others who may become your support system. Having a familiar face in a big meeting can be a real confidence booster and keep you grounded.

Try to learn about the cultural norms and stakeholder management as soon as you start at a new job. In absence of an Organizational Network Analysis (ONA), that would give you a map of influencers in the organization. Observe the behavior of leaders whose attributes and actions are aligned to your values. These are the leaders you can learn from to enhance your leadership skills and navigate new roles. They might be the best mentors for you, and nurturing those relationships is your responsibility.

In your first month in a new group, demonstrate your ability to adapt to ever-changing demands of a dynamic organization. You might start a project with clear goals, only to find that internal and external factors can shift the team's objectives. Sometimes, even experts may not be the best guides, and decision-makers might take paths you don't fully agree with. The type of team you join will define how work gets done. In Agile teams, everyone has equal opportunities to voice their opinion and ideas for collective goals, guided by Agile coaches and scrum-masters that know how to harvest the best out of each team member. During daily stand-ups, team members freely share what has been done, what needs to be completed and what help they need to accomplish these goals. In a self-directed team, all members are leading toward a common goal with shared accountability. In addition to these practices, modern blended and distributed teams may choose to progress their mission asynchronously, and this might be another approach you may need to adapt to and maybe adopt. But that's not necessarily how all companies choose to deploy teams. When selecting your next employer, make sure to ask how work gets done and how cross-functional teams work together. Agile ways of working are the norm for top-notch companies.

To become a great team member, you might want to ask about team norms and preferred styles of communication. Feeling like you belong to the team is one of the most rewarding results of a well-managed working group. Knowing that you are contributing, are respected, and heard is ultimately how all members should engage in teamwork. Being a team player means that you know when to hold your own ideas back in service of others and vice versa.

So far, I have been focusing on how to develop leadership skills from the start of your career and how self-awareness will help you learn new habits.

Within the framework of consciousness, curiosity, and courage, you can begin to deconstruct the leadership of the future into components of human abilities, skills, behaviors, preferences, biological pre-dispositions, cultural backgrounds, and personal identities. To do this, let's dive into the skills that are now essential for a successful career. It may seem overwhelming at first, but work has been rapidly changing, with technology and capabilities growing faster than ever. This transformation requires a workforce that can keep up, allowing businesses to meet the needs of their customers, stakeholders, and employees by providing personalized experiences. This new reality by itself is creating a huge pressure in organizations depending on highly skilled workers to maintain high performance and deliver on their business plans. The workforce is always evolving, and the workplace must adapt to meet both individual needs and teamwork demands. Achieving this balance is the secret to leading a successful organization.

Now, let's think about your perspective on work. Just a few years ago, you were probably pondering work/life balance, realizing that it didn't quite fit your reality. Next came work/life integration, where work and personal life coexisted, but it didn't always consider your individual needs and preferences. Now, everyone is buzzing about work/life harmonization, a more flexible approach. It's about figuring out your various roles as a productive member of society and how work fits into your life. It's up to you to assess where, how, and what you do professionally, and these choices might not be straightforward. Talking to trusted friends can be a big help in finding your way.

There are many ways to work, so it's crucial to figure out what suits you, your work style, and your preferences. Some may prefer diving deep into a specific passion as an independent professional for the freedom it offers, while others might thrive in various full-time roles and organizations. Your choice depends on factors like job security, your comfort with organizational dynamics, adaptability to formal structures, benefits, and more. Economic conditions, global events, and your personal life milestones can also play a role. But today, you have more options, from independent contracting to informal agreements, making work experiences richer. In the future, switching between different roles and contracts across organizations will become more common. So, find what fits for you and stay updated on industry trends.

Broadly speaking, the jobs you choose to pursue are reflections of who you are. Situational employment may be part of the journey when you're limited by choices and must work for survival as was my case when I first arrived in the US. However, your curiosity and courage to try new ways of working may pleasantly surprise you. I recall the time I was working in restaurants as an immigrant with limited English. One of my first customers as a waiter was actress Faye Dunaway at the American Festival Café. Having misunderstood her order, I brought her the wrong drink, and a salad with dressing on it, which apparently was a terrible mistake. I learned my lesson and waited on tables for many years, sometimes working three shifts in different restaurants to make ends meet, and I am proud of mastering that job and making a good living with it. Your journey might surprise you, too.

The road to a great job is not always clear and the detours that will come your way may help you gain valuable unplanned experiences and skills. This is a perfect moment for us to take a detour to explore the opportunities available to you, whoever you are, or whatever school you attended. This section is for anyone interested in the discovery of a professional trajectory that may not be a linear roadmap, and is seeking a gratifying career. In fact, the most interesting jobs may have nothing to do with the level or compensation we so often dream about. This shift in mindset is a key ingredient in unlocking your potential and finding the flow of work that emerges from consciousness, curiosity, and courage as you build your leadership skills. To begin your reflection, stay present and sit comfortably. Close your eyes for a few minutes and breathe as in previous exercises. Start by envisioning your ideal work, workplace (digital, remote, physical), and envision what you're doing, including who you're working with. This scenario helps you get in touch with what you really want to experience. Repeat this exercise as often as you can as it is shaping your intention, and focus on real life. Write down some insights and continue to focus on how you position yourself to be at your best.

As a civilization, we are entering a new phase in awareness, consciousness and dare I say, emotional and spiritual well-being. In this collective movement towards learning, accepting, and sharing our lives in groups, we're developing the ability to stay present, appreciate our current space and time with humility. This is not to say you don't get frustrated or upset at work for things that are beyond your control. Those moments, however, provide you with an opportunity to assess your approach, and the chance to reframe the situation to better manage it. This is the secret of great leaders: they know their triggers and respond with an observer's view of the situation. Knowing thyself is always the first step in handling emotionally charged situations. In teams and groups, this is even more important as you go through difficult conversations with an open heart and mind, to listen and assess what's best for the well-being of the group. In teams, all members play a role in asking questions that drive progress. Building relationships isn't always easy, and sometimes, you'll need to learn how to forgive and move past upsetting events as they happen.

Think about a time when someone irritated you at work. Describe it in your own words and allow yourself to have the most instinctive emotional reaction. You may even curse a bit to let out the negative energy. Now that you worked yourself up, close your eyes for a moment to focus on the present, let thoughts about those involved come and go like the clouds in the sky. Focus on breathing slowly and deeply, in and out as the oxygen is nurturing you with love. Tell yourself that you are talented and lovable, that you love yourself and accept your traits and your flaws, without judgment. Not easy, right? Your thoughts jump back into the memory with blame towards those who made you feel bad. You probably got stuck in being right, while others are wrong. But now, try to let go of that need to be right. Understand that the situation is in the past, and those people probably felt the consequences of their actions. Remember, it's human to carry past experiences into new ones. Close your eyes again and tell yourself to release those negative emotions. Forgive yourself and others for any misunderstandings and mistaken assumptions. Shift your thoughts to how beautiful you are and how right here, right now, everything is okay. Stay present. Let go and move on. You might want to wish them well.

It's not comfortable, I know, but worth the practice. Leaders learn to accept reality and figure out how to respond to all the stuff life throws at them by focusing on the best possible options. It's not magic, but there are a few human development and psychological things you should know to really make sense of your life experiences and become more emotionally savvy.

You're on a continuous path of growth that calls for a bunch of sensory skills and an open mind to find new meanings in what life throws your way. And remember, you're not on this journey alone. You've got to learn how to navigate life in working teams with confidence. One of the best habits you can develop as you journey towards great leadership is observing others with a friendly smile, showing your curiosity and acceptance of them.

Neuroscience and human behavior research have unveiled the complexities of how we react, express ourselves, and communicate. I recently watched a video of someone talk about coming out as gay to their parents. In just a minute, you could see their emotions shift from happiness to sadness and fear. They instinctively closed their jacket, like a protective shield. This quick and dramatic transformation is common in our lives as we're often on the lookout for potential dangers, reactions from others, and responses to what we say or think.

Now, as a leader, you'll need to be super aware of these signals from others. You've got to quickly figure out what you can say or do based on your intention and their readiness to receive your message. Being intentional in your actions and communication is a superpower, but the real secret to effective communication is sensing how open your audience is to your message. This skill involves reading the collective mindset and it's a game-changer.

Team effectiveness is a collective accountability.

Coaching yourself to succeed is mostly an exercise in self-determination, discipline, and the openness to learn and grow towards your personal goals. But here's the deal, when you start your job, you're also entering a community of people working in different teams and structures. It's like a whole new world of human interactions. One of the secrets of working well in teams and groups is to observe, listen, and learn for the clues to see what kind of relationships are being formed within the business context. This is especially important as others are also trying to assess what kind of person you are. Allow for the energy between you to be positive.

You may discover that you share more similarities than differences in how you react to new places, people, and projects. These events may scare you, but as you probably already know from experience, the anticipation is usually worse than reality. Meeting new people in new places and being assigned to new projects have great impact on most of us. Stay in the now. Don't compare past experiences with what's happening in the moment. Instead, see them as fresh chances to be the leader you aspire to be. Take a piece of paper and describe the leader you would like to be in the third person. This process helps you solidify your intention in becoming someone you are proud of and feel respect for.

Be comfortable with the gradual progress you will make in shaping your professional persona, building your brand, and getting in touch with your most authentic self. You are not immune to others' ideals and perceptions of you. What builds your resilience is a foundational belief that you have the coping skills, the ability to solve dilemmas and gain support from those you have a positive relationship with. In the workplace, you will need to assess your network of colleagues and teammates, and share your vulnerabilities, your fears, and your feelings so you can develop emotional connections with them. This intimacy is real and provides you with an opportunity to build a group of people you can count on when you need the support of friends. Life at work is a series of encounters, conversations, exchanges, overt and covert communications, and experiences that will require your attention, your appreciation, and sometimes your forgiveness.

Regardless of the work arrangement you're in, emotions will arise when you least expect it. Suppose you're all set to speak with your boss on a Zoom call. You have dressed yourself up, fixed your hair, sent the dog to another room, and chosen a background that hides the messy room you are in . . . just to realize your boss decided to stay off-camera today. You immediately question if you should also be off camera, or should you pretend all is okay and move forward with the meeting with this uncomfortable feeling that your boss didn't respect you enough to be on camera, which of course is just an assumption. Now you can't see her non-verbal reactions. Where do you look now? At her black square? At the camera? This can trigger reactions, feelings, and doubts, especially when they are your subordinates, and you're not explicitly discussing it. And this is just one example of how you can become preoccupied with peripheral thoughts and may send the wrong signals. The secret is clarity. Just because you can be on camera, doesn't mean it's a camera day for the person you are talking to.

Humans seek control of their environment; physical and emotional safety are often our primary concerns in organizational work life. We quickly assign labels to others as if we could find a place for every person in our mind just by looking at them. This is extremely harmful when you are in groups that must work together and share experiences. I recall when I was an Employee Assistance Program (EAP) counselor and a female professional from a global company called the hotline to say she was afraid she was going to get fired. She said she was not sleeping at night due to her daughter's mental illness, but felt ashamed of sharing that with her boss, who apparently had been friendly and supportive over the years. The caller stated that she was falling asleep in meetings and was told that it was unacceptable behavior. No one asked her if she was having any issues or showed her any empathy. She was ashamed of the situation and became isolated in her department. This could have been managed much better if her supervisor had approached her with kindness and asked if there was anything interfering with her work. These narratives are most often generated inside our brains using impulsive response systems to stimuli. That's why it is so important to learn about our psychological processes, states of well-being, and even disorders that may be impacting our social lives at work. The best option in most of these situations is to communicate, provide clarity, and connect with the intention to understand.

For most employees, the workplace is an uncertain environment where things are continuously changing, people are moving in and out, and our roles, positions and projects are being assessed for the value they create for the organization. Employees are concerned about their year-end performance assessments, potential layoffs, and a myriad of risks associated with being a full-time employee. These stressors can have a negative impact on workers who are under pressure to provide for their families. These pervasive thoughts, reactions, fears, and emotions are having a negative impact on the culture of an organization, and they must be understood to be managed appropriately. An insensitive manager, leader, or colleague can cause emotional distress in others without the awareness of their impact. The efforts currently being enacted in companies to de-stigmatize mental health is helping people recognize that seeking mental health services and focusing on your well-being are practices that lead to better outcomes in business. Most organizations are offering benefits related to physical, emotional, and professional wellness.

Learning to work with others will improve your ability to be a solid team member and a leader who is well equipped to handle all kinds of situations. In a team, the interpersonal dynamics can become quite prominent, often leading to conflicts and misunderstandings during meetings. But it is important to know that effective teams require team norms. And you can be seen as a leader just for suggesting learning about how you want to work together and establish some team norms.

Another important conversation that teams should have as they embark on a mission is about decision-making processes. This conversation is essential for agility and achieving the best outcomes, and ties into prioritization. It's also important to call out if the team seems to be avoiding a conversation about something that's not working. This is the most difficult conversation to have with team members, but the topic must be raised respectfully and discussed as an intervention for the team to work more effectively.

Another important conversation for your growth involves discussing what you've learned as a team. Having a dialogue about insights gained during teamwork sessions and how they impacted performance and team dynamics is crucial for developing a team culture that continuously improves and involves everyone in building better relationships. Talking about what you've learned together will support candor, feedback, and ultimately make everyone even better team members for the next project. These discussions about team effectiveness and performance are the foundation of organizational success and a positive work culture. While they may be challenging, they also enhance your leadership skills, which can be valuable in environments where open dialogue isn't yet the norm, and team coaching is recognized as a necessary component.

CHAPTER 10

Becoming a People Leader

Embrace the manager role.

Become a People Leader, a pivotal role that allows you to positively impact people's work experiences and contribute to an organization's growth. Leading others is a personal achievement, and the preparation for a manager position starts on your first day as an individual contributor. The experience of reporting to someone new, the understanding of the interpersonal dynamics shaping the workplace, and your own journey as an employee, will provide you with the knowledge to begin your training as a People Leader, which in this book I refer to as the new role of the manager in future-ready organizations. As part of your discovery, it will be important to observe good leaders who show interest in their people's well-being and career growth, while leading high performing teams and delivering results. Alternatively, it is good to understand the negative impact leaders can have on their people when they're unable to empathize or connect with their reports. Being a People Leader involves developing a deep appreciation for human connections and recognizing the unique complexities of individuals in the workplace. Your role is to influence organizational systems and create an environment where team members can thrive and deliver their best work.

Leading others is a privilege, not a right. It is easy to think you can follow processes and standard communications to lead a productive team. However, the world of work has dramatically changed, and the ways in which you could manage employees in the past are no longer relevant. The workplace is multi-generational, diverse, and incredibly difficult to navigate for leaders who have not done the work to reflect on themselves and listen to others. If you aspire to become a People Leader, you can start by seeing others as unique individuals with potential for growth. Although the role of the manager is changing, there are immutable skills you will need to develop for building trust, human-centric leadership, and coaching direct reports. The art of feedback will be imperative for you as you become a People Leader, but the skills to build a team that collectively care for each other, share values and purpose, might be the highest level of leadership you can aspire to achieve.

In my experience as the global leader of management development for thousands of managers at different levels of maturity, I believe People Leaders have three key responsibilities: Team Performance, Career Coaching, and Community Development. There is a continuous debate about the role of the manager versus the role of the leader, and I strongly believe that People Leaders must acquire leadership skills and exercise them from the start. The word "manager" doesn't reflect what the position demands of these leaders, and it seems archaic to label these amazing coaches and high performing professionals with that title. In fact, People Leaders are no longer managing their team members on a day-to-day basis, as team members need autonomy, and often are working in cross-functional and Agile teams. In the new workplace, the People Leader must be the custodian of the enterprise values, a champion of cultural norms, and an excellent coach, and team leader whose inspiration, thought leadership, creativity and focus on prioritization will lead their team to success. In this context, the People Leader is the architect of the employee experience and a source of positive energy invoking ambidextrous skills in navigating market shifts, organizational strategy as well as attracting, retaining, and developing talent.

Be a conscious People Leader.

Moving from an individual contributor to a People Leader is a big shift. Employees will expect your guidance, support, coaching, recognition, appreciation, feedback, and care. The transition demands self-awareness and a deeper reflection on your own issues from previous roles to avoid repeating mistakes. If you struggled to empathize with teammates or co-workers in the past, when you become a People Leader you will be challenged to learn interpersonal skills. In addition, it is becoming increasingly more difficult to create personalized employee experiences in a world where uncertainty and ambiguity are pervasive. The role of the People Leader is to offer hope, provide safety, help your team become resilient, and develop adaptive coping skills. To succeed in this new role, you must prioritize your team and act with empathy, even when making tough business decisions.

The conscious People Leader has mastered self-management, ensuring their biases, personal agendas, ambition, and fears are kept in check, while serving their teams and organizations. In today's world of work, People Leaders will need to maintain a diverse network of internal relationships, external contacts, and partners to understand their industries, their organizational goals, and learn how work is being done across the company. Yes, it sounds like a difficult role to play, but as we will see in the next pages, its key responsibilities can be summarized in a People Leader Profile composed of human, organizational, and digital abilities under the Leadership Expressions: Consciousness, Curiosity, and Courage. These fundamental aspects of great leadership are vital in any organization adapting its systems to empower its people, working together to achieve clear business strategies and growth as a community of skilled professionals and leaders.

The future-ready People Leader must be adept at reading market trends, understanding industry evolution, and aligning with their organization's direction while keeping their team's priorities in focus. Additionally, they need to grasp capacity and resource management to strategize for the adaptable twenty-first century workforce, which is characterized as Distributed, Dynamic, Digital, Diverse, and Discerning, as discussed earlier. People Leaders must excel at decision-making to access the talent cost-effectively through strategic workforce planning and creative solutions for the evolving skill-based economy.

Distributed and Digital: lead the new workforce ecosystem.

The concept of leading a workforce that's mostly distributed and digital is still new. It may take a decade or so for organizations to fully leverage the new workforce composition. This new workforce includes not only full-time employees, but also independent professionals, open talent–community members, professional partners, fractional experts, consultants, and various combinations of skilled individuals available in the job market. The liberation of the workforce from the constraints of commuting distances and physical proximity to co-workers, is transforming the notion of what is the workplace. Distributed teams are fully utilizing digital tools to reduce the distance between themselves and their peers, the organization, customers, and the work itself. To stay ahead of the curve, a People Leader must be fluent in navigating these tools, utilizing technology whenever possible, and be adept at communicating with team members. Understanding this is vital because regulatory bodies are increasingly concerned about the nature of engagements professionals accept from large organizations. These engagements must align with employment and privacy laws, making it essential for People Leaders to navigate these waters effectively.

The distributed workforce is here to stay, and as you learn to embrace it, you will discover new experiences that enhance your teams' ability to achieve outcomes faster. This is due to developing connected communities of knowledge and leading through talent ecosystems. The distributed workforce allows for companies to strategically plan talent and skills access from a variety of sources that will offer the greatest opportunity for the development of inclusive teams and a diverse skilled workforce. To build a strong culture and lead the organization through people, companies will need to solve for the lack of proximity to their employees and find new ways to connect with their teams through digital and virtual channels. For front line workers, however, these changes have a different impact which is compounded with a low unemployment rate in the US, and low wages.

The distributed workforce is a digital workforce. Since the early 2000s, organizations have embarked on the Digital Transformation of their businesses to match customers' expectations, respond to market shifts, and accelerate the transition to commercial grade platforms and technologies that could offer them new capabilities and a competitive advantage across industries, globally. Most companies moved to hybrid, private and/or public cloud environments to ensure business continuity through major disruptions. Robotic Process Automation (RPA), machine learning, artificial intelligence (AI), Internet of Things (IOT), Blockchain, Business Analytics, and the exponential proliferation of tools and technologies became integral components of the virtual enterprise. Recent emergence of Generative AI and Large Language Models (LLM), and trained technologies are challenging organizations to adopt new ways of thinking, acquiring knowledge, and simplifying their operations as well as developing intelligent content management systems.

As a People Leader, it's essential to keep up with the latest technologies your team is exploring. The new tools will speed work up, and there may be risks and advantages to early adopters of new applications. Your organization will establish ethical guidelines for using AI, but technology will likely advance faster than you can evaluate its pros and cons. In addition, a People Leader maintains equal access to resources and tools for the multi-generational workforce. It will be a challenge for People Leaders to stay current on the best digital platforms and channels. And this is why it will be so critical for People Leaders to be trained on technology, analytics, and tools to attain digital fluency and catch up with their teams' level. Furthermore, People Leaders are to define strategy for their people with clarity of direction and goals, including upskilling and reskilling initiatives.

In the 2020s, the physical workplace very quickly became a virtual experience. This was a turning point in the distributed and digital characteristics of the new workforce. Post-pandemic, most organizations adapted their people strategies to match the needs of their employees and communities at large. The desire to return employees to a physical workspace didn't materialize as originally planned by business executives, and the new workforce with newly acquired digital skills became even more productive working from afar. The Future of Work arrived without any long-term planning from executive committees who lacked experience in managing a digital environment, asynchronous work, and the distribute workforce, which is also very dynamic.

The human impact of these massive changes is still unclear, but it's fair to assume that the rise in mental health complaints among younger generations is a sign that we must pay attention to how people are connecting and relating to each other at work. As a People Leader you will need to develop skills for dealing with mental challenges. Mental health professionals spend many years developing them to avoid their own burn out. People Leaders are not trained as clinicians and shouldn't attempt to become one; however, learning about human behavior and emotional development might be a way to mitigate the pervasive mental health crisis of this century. Further, Human Resources professionals are not equipped to manage these situations, yet. This is why HR is revising essential skills to replace old traditional processes with more dynamic and human centered abilities.

You are probably questioning the value of becoming a People Leader and whether you want to stay away from this responsibility. I would ask you to reflect, discuss the topic with those who have been in the role, and begin to contemplate mastering these leadership skills without the burden of perfection. Becoming a People Leader is a step towards consciousness and growth. You will learn from interactions and be even better at handling conflicts and relationships, which in turn will help you feel more confident as you realize that it is not about knowing, but the ability to stay present, listen with intention, co-creating coping skills and being open to new experiences. People have been experiencing difficulties in socializing after the pandemic and the implications to early-in-career professionals is unfolding as we learn how to reintegrate ourselves in the social fabric of the workplace. Some are experiencing social anxiety after starting their careers virtually, others are feeling the loneliness with remote work, and a third segment is trying to recover their old ways of working to regain a sense of normalcy. As a People Leader, your role is to empathize with multiple realities to find new ways of engaging and inspiring your people to create a better future.

Dynamic & Diverse: rethink talent strategy.

It is undeniable that organizations focused on developing a diverse workforce and an inclusive workplace are advancing their strategies faster, producing more innovative products and solutions, as well as building a more positive business reputation in the marketplace. Customers are demanding transparency in how their communities are being represented within the corporations that serve them. From supplier diversity to real progress towards equity and advancement of underrepresented minorities, organizations are taking their role in society more seriously as their public image is as important as the quality of their products and services. The best companies are making progress in creating equity in opportunities for all employees to grow and advance in their careers.

However, the reality of our current global business environment, uncertain economy, and generational shifts in attitudes toward old norms, are forcing organizations to rethink their talent strategies by accepting that the new workforce is diverse, but also very dynamic. As described in previous pages, millennials going through the 2008 financial crisis quickly realized that career velocity was a personal responsibility, and the fastest way to enhance their financial wellness was through external mobility. This reality has transformed how organizations prioritize the employee experience and the career growth of their best talent. The current members of this dynamic workforce are leaving their jobs after 18–36 months in search of better opportunities, new skills, and higher compensation. In fact, some reports state that compensation has become a top priority for them.

Don't be discouraged by the new trends in workforce dynamics. As a People Leader you will be able to wow your people and create an incomparable employee experience by being authentic and empowering. Besides, societal changes are beyond your control, and the fact that the workforce is now dynamic means that our talent strategies must follow suit. In my experience working with major organizations and thousands of people, I have learned that it is imperative that companies execute on a flawless three-year dynamic talent strategy. In the first year, employees need to know they belong, which requires great on-boarding plans, human connection, and coaching. People Leaders will be focused on creating the best second year for the employee who needs to know the company is invested in them. This will demand a skills assessment, career conversations, and a growth plan for the employee. The third year is a defining moment in one's career, as the organization assesses the individual as a potential member of their leadership pipeline, and employees assess their chances of progressing in the organization before making alternative plans to move.

In addition to the new dynamics in the workplace, workers are more diverse than ever before, and the dimensions of their identities are topics of discussions, programs and policies in leadership meetings, and Human Resources departments. The future workplace must be truly inclusive, and businesses must accelerate the growth opportunities available to underrepresented communities to build a more engaged workforce. Companies should aim to place diverse leaders in visible roles and create equity. As a People Leader you will need to reflect deeply on your own beliefs regarding minority groups and allow for new knowledge to inform your decisions.

As you entertain the opportunity to lead a culture of inclusion and equity, you might want to learn a few ways in which organizations can optimize their talent strategies and solutions in service of a more pragmatic plan of action. As a People Leader, your role involves delving into Strategic Workforce Planning. This means assessing current and future skills needs, forecasting roles, and guiding employees and leaders through development. This has been a Human Resources responsibility that must be shared with business leaders. In summary, People Leaders will need to expand their abilities to lead value-driven business strategies while maintaining a high performing team and leading the employee experience to ensure their retention as well as adapt to the skill-based economy.

Employees are Discerning: don't underestimate the intelligence of your people.

Today's workforce stands out for its ability to make informed choices. They've seen the instability of full-time jobs and the myth of lifelong loyalty to a single company. Entering the job market, early-in-career professionals are discovering new ways of participating in the economy and exploring opportunities. These professionals are also rethinking work/life balance and aligning their values with career decisions. And this is a positive development in our society that's now replacing blind dedication to an employer with a more balanced ambition that integrates work with their lives and purpose.

Work in the flow of life.

The manifestation of a new collective consciousness is enhancing our awareness of the need for action in the creation of a sustainable economy when science is providing us with the clear threats to our livelihood as humans. We face challenges like global warming, pollution, resource scarcity, water shortages, and the consequences of industrialization. These concerns are prompting individuals and organizations to reflect, make thoughtful choices, and take action. Today's organizations must be cognizant of their role in decreasing these risks or contributing to the problems. Professionals today are reevaluating their career paths, seeking success while upholding integrity and environmental responsibility. From social justice to inclusion to regenerative initiatives and world peace, employers and employees are taking accountability for the future and realigning their priorities towards sustainability and growth.

When everything seems to be in question, it is natural to infer that organizations are struggling to make sense of a complex business ecosystem that's interconnected through global channels of supply management, production, and delivery of services, offerings, and products. The value chain must be reorganized within old parameters, and companies are taking steps to design new operating systems while working on growing profitably and being disrupted by new competitors, technology, social concerns, and humanitarian crisis. As a leader, your focus is on making sense of this complex environment and providing clarity for yourself, your peers, and your entire team. It is an exciting time to be a People Leader, as your positive impact can ripple out and help shape a better world through conscious actions and the use of your influence.

The process of leadership development is gradual and non-linear. There will be days you will feel you are not up for the role of a People Leader; other days you will feel empowered to support your teams and engage them in meaningful conversations. The key to great leadership is to allow for self-care and support from others so you can recharge. This is a critical point: You can't rescue others from their experiences and life situations, but you can listen, witness their stories, empathize with them, and provide support. Often, when facing others' struggles, we wish to solve their problems, but unfortunately, it's not always possible. As a great leader, you can offer a safe space for a person, free of judgment.

From competition to collaboration: contribute to the collective intelligence.

It is important to emphasize the distinction between leading your professional success as an individual contributor and building your reputation and value as a People Leader. You were probably told that to win in business, you need to focus on your goals and relentlessly pursue them. But the role of a People Leader is measured by team-based metrics such as low voluntary attrition, team diversity, attainment of business targets, productive collaboration, level of engagement, skills, and the overall business outcomes. A People Leader will have followers in the organization due to sharing power, role modeling behaviors that elevate their teams, and by building a positive reputation. This will increase your social capital and help you advance in your career.

You may have the impulse to demonstrate your knowledge above all else, but you don't want to earn a reputation of a know-it-all. This is one of the challenges of People Leaders that deserves consideration. Your team members need to know you trust them in their ability to find ways to problem solve. Your job is to respond to their needs and offer expert guidance, but not solutions.

And this is the perfect time to talk about your Personal Success Profile to deconstruct the role of the future-ready leader. In my career, I've seen leadership trends that come and go, with debates about models, competencies, behaviors, and attributes. While it's important to expand your knowledge of these theories, I believe in the lasting importance of core leadership skills. Leadership is a transformative process of self-discovery that requires a mindset of self-knowledge and a deeper understanding of human behavior in preparation to acquire those skills. These leadership qualities provide a blueprint of the leader of the future. Furthermore, the skills described here are essentially human traits that will help you grow personally and professionally to lead a fulfilling life.

CHAPTER 11

Developing your Personal Success Profile (PSP)

Express outstanding leadership for your success.

Before diving into the human capabilities and skills of future-ready leaders, it is important to reiterate the three Cs of your character and their corresponding leadership expressions:

> **Consciousness = Being**
> **Curiosity = Seeking**
> **Courage = Doing**

Consciousness = Being

Discover your beliefs and transform them into authentic expressions of who you want to be.

Exercise: As you read about this leadership expression and start exploring *being*, please write a paragraph describing the leader you want to be. I want you to create your individual leadership manifesto using "I"-statements that describe who you are, what your purpose is, and how you pledge to show up as a leader. Enjoy the ride!

Curiosity = Seeking

Discover new ideas and learn about the world of others to ignite innovation and collective success.

 Exercise: For this exercise, think about your curiosity as an innate drive to explore. Many leaders I coach start by saying "I'm not creative" or may say "I'm not good with technology." These are self-limiting beliefs we use to tackle the stress of trying new things. Remember that your curiosity must be cultivated through learning. Identify things that you have formed opinion about and train your brain to be open to new ideas. Welcome this opportunity to grow and learn. Seek the unknown! For this exercise you might choose a culture, a country, or an ethnic group that you wish to learn more about.

Courage = Doing

Discover your strengths and act with the belief that you hold the power to change the world.

 Exercise: Sit quietly and try to recall a situation or event that triggered your fears, but you dealt with anyway. What were the lessons learned in that act of courage? Did you feel relieved once the event was over, and did that event help you build courage for future situations? After reflecting on what you've learned, move toward your current context, and identify issues that you might be afraid of addressing. Think about what's making you feel that you can't act in alignment with your beliefs. Is someone else making this difficult for you?

Name the fear, ask yourself why is it there? After that, create a plan of action. It is empowering, and you can always see it as an experiment. It is amazing what you can discover once you acknowledge your fears. This is the first step in building courage. It is about building belief.

Build your Personal Success Profile (PSP).

To make it easy, think about the acronym CARDS as the five essential skills you need to be successful in a new workplace. In a sense, you will be asked to show your CARDS to be noticed, valued, and seen as a leader. Showing up fully at the workplace and being authentic in your interactions, you will play your CARDS with transparency to reach your aspirations. Let's explore each of the Leadership Skills comprising your PSP:

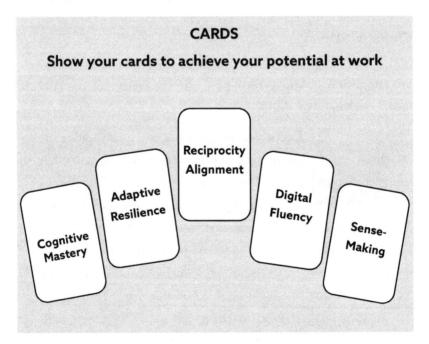

CARDS

Show your cards to achieve your potential at work

Reciprocity Alignment

Adaptive Resilience

Digital Fluency

Cognitive Mastery

Sense-Making

CARDS: Your license to win in the new world.

Cognitive Mastery

- Self-management
- Communications
- Critical Thinking

Adaptive Resilience

- Continuous Learning
- Empathy & Compassion
- Energy Management

Reciprocity Alignment

- Interpersonal Sensitivity
- Inclusive Networking
- Teaming & Sharing

Digital Fluency

- Ethical Agility
- Creativity
- Systems Thinking

Sense-Making

- Signal Seeking
- Business Literacy
- Analytical Thinking

Cognitive Mastery:

Self-Management, Communications and Critical Thinking

We've discussed the way you respond to emotional stimuli and how to do it in more productive ways. You have already discovered that emotions can quickly take over. You can overcome this by training your brain through a conscious effort to try and become your best self. In this context, Cognitive Mastery means that you become aware of your instant emotional reactions to triggers, acknowledging them and catching yourself in time. This allows your thinking brain (prefrontal cortex) to step in, process your reactions more logically and more appropriately. It is very difficult, but it is critical for leaders to respond without getting overwhelmed by emotions, but also to navigate the complex and often contradictory realities of our world. Cognitive Mastery also means the ability to absorb data, gain insights, manage biases, and make sense of the world through effective communications and critical thinking.

Cognitive Mastery is a higher-level skill that demands mindful attention to your impulses, preconceived ideas, and self-limiting beliefs that shape your Critical Thinking and understanding of new situations. To start training your brain in this skill, you should reflect on situations in which you made hasty decisions about something that could've been better handled with cognitive mastery. This skill also involves recognizing the external and internal pressures you place on yourself to meet expectations without much thought. Essentially, it encourages you to slow down, identify the triggers in a situation, and respond thoughtfully and diplomatically. To develop this skill, practice gathering information, gaining insights, using intuition while being aware of your preferences and emotions, and seeking feedback from trusted sources. This will help you become more adept at thinking before acting and making informed decisions.

Your Personal Success Profile (PSP) has a wide-reaching impact and involves various aspects of development. An essential skill related to Cognitive Mastery is self-awareness. Being aware helps you understand the complexities of human behavior by consciously striving to empathize and interpret emotions, both in yourself and in others. This is also about the ability to hold multiple realities as sources of data, avoiding attachment to self-limiting beliefs, and presenting yourself authentically. This process involves observing without immediately reacting, which allows you to respond as a leader with composure and poise. Note that rationalization is not Cognitive Mastery. To enhance your maturity and cognition, you should blend your Self-Management skills, Critical Thinking abilities, and Communication skills to maintain a nonjudgmental stance, formulate thoughtful responses, and express yourself with confidence.

Communicating is how you manifest your value.

Excellent oral and written communications are building blocks of a leader's influence. This is important for leadership developing at all levels. It becomes even more valuable, when you're leading an organization, a community, or a movement. Whether you're leading a team, a department, a business unit, or a region within a company, your words carry a certain energy that can be contagious. To be a great communicator, focus on delivering messages that are clear and easily understood, along with the reasons behind them. Make sure everyone in your audience knows what's expected of them. Great communicators possess self-awareness and a keen sense of how others receive their messages. They are quick to pause, adjust if needed, and manage their energy to ensure their messages are purposeful and valuable.

A message that's delivered with purpose has a positive impact on people and has the power to influence how people perceive and engage with the topics at hand. Leaders who nurture compassion and believe in their ideas, can spontaneously speak to inspire, provide comfort, or offer reassurance during a crisis, with authenticity. To communicate effectively, you will need to believe in your ability to motivate others and be humble enough to seek help in crafting your messages. Often, corporate messaging is carefully curated by communication experts to minimize disruption and avoid unexpected negative reactions. On the other hand, some leaders may command attention but lack empathy, delivering information in a cold, offensive manner that alienates their audience. The key is to strike a balance between connecting with your audience, showing vulnerability, and stating your message with clarity, integrity, and courage. And remember that most leaders overestimate their abilities, so it's wise to test your messages with your network to find even better ways to connect with your audience.

Communicating with purpose is about learning to be realistic without being aggressive, to communicate sensitive content clearly, and delivering a personal message responsibly and considerately. When great leaders speak both from their minds and hearts, their audience listens with respect, creating a shared experience that transcends the good, the bad, and the ugly. The goal of great speeches is to unite people. Many corporate leaders understand that expressing genuine emotions can have a significantly positive impact on how their message is received. Written communications must be crafted with care to connect with the reader emotionally, and practically guide them with clarity.

Exercise: Write a speech for yourself and practice it by recording it, or as an alternative, you can use an app to transcribe an impromptu speech. To start the process, think about a topic that's important to you and could be as important to others in your community. Just for fun, let's imagine that you have been invited to deliver a short keynote during a community meeting in your organization. The meeting is celebrating teamwork and collaboration. Assess who is in the audience and use a Design Thinking tool: the Empathy Map, which is basically your understanding of what the designated persona feels, say, do and think about this topic. This helps you to be attuned to the people you will speak to. You can choose an individual contributor, a new member of the team, diversity group members, managers, leaders, or any other segment of the workforce. Then, decide what they would want to hear from you. You are a People Leader in that community, and your team members are in the audience. What do you need to say that resonates with you, the team, and everyone else? How can you be vulnerable and authentic while showing your leadership to inspire their growth? Use pauses, short powerful sentences, and breathe calmly while looking at the camera, or directly at the center of an auditorium, and say what you need to say. Pay attention to your body language. Try not to move side to side, or squeeze your hands, rather just stand up straight with arms down at your sides and deliver the speech. It will be fun, and you can grow into a confident speaker. Don't be too critical of yourself and watch the video with empathy. In addition to your practice, you can look up speaking tips and get guidance in many learning channels online. The idea is to create value by doing something that's not yet comfortable.

Adaptive Resilience:

Continuous Learning, Empathy & Compassion, Energy Management

Throughout your career, you will encounter countless opposing forces coming from seemingly opposite directions. Your task is to comprehend and synthesize these complexities so that others can grasp them. To reach this level of thinking, you will rely on your Cognitive Mastery skills and empathy to avoid making judgments before you understand the origins of your perspective. And this is how you build resilience as a leader. The ability to pause before responding, witnessing people's experiences without rescuing them, tolerating potential criticism from others, and the experience of failure, are all learning opportunities for you to develop resilience as a leader. This ability to adapt is particularly useful in environments where company interests, employees' values, customer demands, and shareholder expectations may not be strategically aligned.

These skills must be continuously learned, and Adaptive Resilience is a set of skills acquired overtime. Polarity management is a key skill for leaders who must navigate radical thoughts, feelings, attitudes, opinions, and position their assessments with a high level of patience to find the best ways to communicate with their communities. It is natural to be in conflict when something challenges your opinion on a specific issue. In some ways, this is how you build Adaptive Resilience, and it helps you identify your biases and pre-conceived notions about people and things. Challenges and openness to new perspectives expand your emotional and cognitive toolkit, providing more options when handling complex situations as a leader. Resilience grows from learning through experiences, allowing others and events to shape your worldview while acknowledging the emotional impact they have on you. Nurturing Adaptive Resilience relies on experiencing the normal emotions tied to loss, grief, compassion, and other emotional expressions. Embracing deeper experiences helps you learn and develop coping skills that contribute to building your resilience.

The adaptive and resilient leader knows that being authentic means acting in line with personal principles, values, and beliefs without disregarding the context and the people involved in unique situations. If you are a leader who has a strong belief and an event is challenging you to think about others' points of view on the subject, you will need to do your best to remain neutral. This concept of agnostic leadership is an aspect you must be comfortable with to increase your effectiveness where not all values and principles are aligned to yours. This delicate balance between your convictions and your commitments to organizational communities is an art you will need to approach with compassion and kindness.

Energy management is a skill for work/life harmonization.

Resilience is not grit. This distinction is important to understand so you don't engage in obsessive behaviors to achieve goals. Resilience is a capability you build that can support your adaptive leadership behaviors in a more mindful way. An adaptive leader must know how to use their social power to advance organizational goals. If there is public outcry and pressure on your organization to respond to political, religious, or even terrorist threats against a given community or protected group, you will need to have the courage to engage, express, and enable responses aligned to your organizational values. However, it may not be well-received in all communities. This is a difficult conflict to manage, but as an adaptive and resilient leader, your commitments supersede personal and/or private risks.

One more skill within Adaptive Resilience is accepting your needs when experiencing demanding emotional situations. Recognizing when you need help and when you might need to care for yourself are important skills of a leader. It seems easy, but it's not. When others are counting on you to support them, make things better, or even to fight for them on a given topic, emotionally you will feel depleted. Adaptive Resilience requires a balance in your life that allows for work/life harmonization without jeopardizing the outcomes you seek. In fact, remaining conscious of your emotional needs, reactions, and difficulties is the greatest level of self-awareness for leaders who know when to step back and see themselves as vulnerable human beings. Leadership in the new workplace is more human centered and does not exclude the leader's holistic well-being. In the future-ready organization, everyone is a leader growing their skills through consciousness, curiosity, and courage. The ability to express emotions and engage followers is a sign of effective leadership according to some studies in social cognitive neuroscience. Staying emotionally connected is engaging and empowering. Remembering that all moments are temporary will strengthen your resilience and solidify your positive coping skills.

 Exercise: Think about a past situation in which you felt that your resilience was being tested. What was the experience and who were the protagonists that made it difficult for you? Remember that you are more objective when reflecting on a situation that has already been resolved. How did you manage your energy? This exercise helps you identify what triggers were present that prevented your adaptive resilience to be activated. We all have vulnerabilities that may interfere with our conscious experiences. You are more likely to adapt your responses and engage in more productive interactions when you know how you may be impacted by certain triggers and events. When you think of times you refrained from saying something you felt strongly about, or you allowed group thinking to go unchecked, ask yourself, what held you back? What thoughts and fears made you decide not to say anything? Navigate new situations while maintaining self-confidence. However, it's important to remember that as humans, we all have moments when we didn't stay true to our beliefs. It takes practice and courage. This exercise is just an attempt to help you become aware of yourself. Finally, think about the last time you allowed yourself to cry. This might give you a sense of how easy or difficult it is for you to be in touch with tough emotions.

Reciprocity Alignment:

Interpersonal Sensitivity, Inclusive Networking, Teaming & Sharing.

Reciprocity Alignment refers to assessing, navigating, and bridging reciprocal actions, communications, and preferences to create harmony in relationships. It is about establishing shared systems of reciprocal behaviors in teams for best collaboration. Fostering reciprocity with an understanding of others' needs at work is becoming one of the most valuable skills in leadership today. Reciprocity

Alignment enables you to seek, nurture, and maintain interpersonal connections with others for mutual gains, respect, and support. It is a continuous process of networking with people outside your affinity groups as a manifestation of an inclusive mindset. To do it well, you will need to develop an ability to enter the emotional experience of others in a nonjudgmental way. This openness to others will help you connect with people and build trust, credibility and share ideas. And as you explore new relationships, participate in social events, identify networking opportunities, and allow yourself to be authentically present, you will be developing a positive personal brand based on your interest in the well-being of others in the community. In addition to a good reputation, you will be building the foundation for teamwork and coaching which are critical skills in growing your career within organizational settings.

Shifting from an individual perspective of success to a collective purpose and teamwork, you will see yourself adding value to an organization's culture. Team is the new unit of value in business environments, and your success depends on how well you master navigating dynamics between team members. Developing interpersonal sensitivity and awareness of nonverbal cues, you will have the opportunity to start your relationships by respecting others' emotional and cognitive states and sharing your leadership. Reciprocity Alignment requires your ability to be inclusive, emotionally attuned to others, and actively listen to divergent reciprocal preferences. Reciprocating based on your own world view may not achieve the results you desire and create an imbalance in your relationships. The idea is to achieve an equilibrium in your relationships by cultivating reciprocity as an organizational cultural norm.

Teaming is your superpower.

It is common for people to use their defenses when entering new environments or meeting new teammates. Defensive mechanisms are mostly subconscious, and it is natural for us to assume comfortable roles in group settings. The key here is to enter new teams and communities in a state of relaxed awareness to avoid repeating old habits. These roles range from the funny person, peacemaker, defiant one, organizer, cynical one, silent one, and to the disruptor, among others. Try to become more aware of the role you tend to play and try new behaviors and habits that may be even more productive in a team setting. Team effectiveness arises from members' conscious discussions about group norms, ways of working and the psychological safety that's created by a leader or the team's collective leadership. Smile, breathe deeply, listen, then calmly express yourself.

You will be part of many groups in your career as a professional individual contributor, or as a manager, or an executive leader. It's inevitable! And learning how teams can achieve the best outcomes is your golden ticket to even better roles and more self-confidence. As I said, we automatically enter new environments with the resources and emotional predispositions from our childhood. If you reflect on the roles you play within your family, you will recognize the similarities in your roles played at work and other areas. Team effectiveness is the result of collective leadership in which members of the team respect each other's ideas, give voice to all members, ask the questions to enhance the team unity, and use positive inquiry to determine how much or how little each member should contribute for successful teamwork. It's important to remember that people might be emotionally triggered and may not show up at their best, and you must consider the fact that what you see is only a moment in time. Getting to know others is an on-going effort.

To boost your Reciprocity Alignment, make sharing your go-to behavior and listening your default skill. This builds trust by showing you're transparent and not hiding information from the team. Sharing is becoming the power skill of the new workplace and being comfortable with the flow of knowledge exchanges with colleagues can greatly enhance your positioning in a company. And as you enter the new era of value creation in business, you will be exploring self-awareness and hopefully the ability to accept feedback without going into defensiveness. It's okay to feel criticized or hurt when people are sharing feedback. Developing interpersonal sensitivity can help you gauge if others are ready to hear your input. This is how you develop relational skills and align your reciprocal actions. You can't control how others choose to express their ideas. The best approach is to accept what they have to say and avoid an impulsive reaction. Take time to absorb the information, consider the context, and respond appropriately. This level of awareness is an asset in your personal and professional growth.

 Exercise: To learn Reciprocity Alignment, as a starting point you will need to reflect on the role you played or still play within your family unit. This is a natural behavior for humans, and it is worth exploring. Take a piece of paper and make two columns with a line. In column A, describe how you see your role in your family (past or present). Think about how you behave during holiday dinners, family gatherings, etc. In column B, reflect on how you usually show up in new groups. How would you describe the role you play in those teams? Have you evolved from your past experiences, and do you have a distinct way in which you collaborate at work? It's likely you will see similarities between the two columns. Now, on a new sheet of paper, describe how you want to show up as a professional team member or leader. Take the opportunity to remind yourself what you need to do to learn new ways of positioning yourself on a team. Reciprocity must be authentic, contextual, and aligned to the current needs of those you interact with. I hope you are proud of who you are becoming! Your intentional interactions will enhance your credibility and contribute to an environment that's psychologically safe.

Digital Fluency:

Ethical Agility, Creativity, and Systems Thinking.

Being tech-savvy is a must in today's workplace. You'll need digital skills to navigate various tools and technologies effectively—from calendars, emails, messaging, file sharing, collaboration tools, automation, and the rapid development of AI and quantum computing, staying up to date is crucial for success. Innovation is happening rapidly, and it's easy to fall behind. Those who embrace technology with curiosity and hunger to learn will thrive, while others may lag. Plus, you'll need to get creative in using AI to enhance your professional career and performance.

No matter your current tech skills, it is in your best interest to keep up with the latest trends. Quantum computing is set to revolutionize the technology development world by 2030, and you'll be the future leader making decisions about its use. For now, however, being digitally adept is a must for tasks and collaborations in a tech-driven workplace. It boosts performance and opens opportunities for learning and innovation. Embracing tools like asynchronous work, can help you coordinate projects more efficiently using technology.

Digital Fluency can improve the way you think and manage, if you are open to exploring new digital tools. Tech skills are driving product development, user experiences, and how employees and customers interact online. This impacts how leaders understand the industry they are in, and connect creativity, co-creation, and business profitability on a large scale. Technology drives transformation in organizations adapting to changing forces. Your digital journey is essential. Knowing how others might use technology in ways that you have not thought of is how innovative companies will gain advantage. Combining your consciousness and curiosity, you will be well equipped to lead these innovative ideas with courage!

Creativity will differentiate you from others.

No pressure, but your creativity and ability to converge multiple sources of inspiration to bring practical value to your organization and its clients will set you apart. Creativity is something we all have but it needs to be nurtured and respected. How many times have you heard yourself or others say, "I am not creative"? I'm sure you are smiling as you read this and can easily recall a few apologetic statements like this. We are all creative, or at least we were all born with the curiosity and ability to try all kinds of experiences during our early childhood. It's well documented in theories of human development that children acquire social cues and mirror their caregivers' actions and behaviors. Children use whatever's available to them to solve the challenges in front of them without questioning whether something is appropriate or helpful. They just follow their instincts and keep on exploring their environment with energy and curiosity. So, if you ever hear someone say they are not creative, you might want to smile, and let them know that maybe they don't feel creative right now, but a little experimentation could turn out to be a wonderful creative discovery.

Why is creativity important in your professional career and leadership journey? Because the best ideas and solutions in business are usually born out of unexpected ways of thinking. "Post-it" became one of the most popular products in the world after its adhesive failed to pass the test of being strong enough for a different purpose, and someone had the creative idea of making use of that weak glue, transforming it into Post-it notes. I hope you know by now that creativity is about giving yourself permission to do great things with freedom. Business leaders and executives are better equipped to manage complex situations when they allow for creative thinking to help them solve these dilemmas. Cultivating a creative mind helps create an environment conducive for innovation. It is not about talent, but an opportunity to rediscover what may have been repressed or discouraged in the process of growing up. In business, creativity might be one of the most critical skills for leaders dealing with an uncertain and volatile world.

 Exercise: Start toying with the tools you have available to explore new advancements you're not aware of. You might ask your preferred Gen AI platform to provide you with a list of innovative technologies that are likely to impact the workplace. You can also ask Generative AI open-source tools to give you examples of team building activities and icebreakers to apply to your next team meeting. In digital marketplaces you can find technologies, partner companies, independent software providers (ISV), and the latest start-ups offering new capabilities that can seamlessly be integrated into your cloud architecture. Explore collaboration tools and enjoy the discoveries you will make. The world of digital tools is expanding quickly, so it might be a good idea to start sooner rather than later.

Sense-Making:

Signal Seeking, Business Literacy, and Analytical Thinking.

You are now entering your unique contribution to a business, and that's an excellent proposition for anyone seeking practical and concrete steps toward leadership success. The art of Sense-Making is what makes this next skill incredibly valuable in business and in life. When so many external variables are simultaneously at play, it is difficult to capture their meaning and impact on the complex web of interconnected organizations. Leaders grapple with the task of distilling the world's complexity into simple, meaningful statements. Researchers analyze data and survey target audiences with control groups and study validity to ensure a more scientific version of whatever is being explored for the publication. However, what we are about to explore is the unique version of the world that great leaders convey as they make sense of what's happening around them. This provides clarity to the people they lead.

Sense-Making is the convergence of art and science within the context of unfolding events and opportunities. As a leader, people look at you with the expectation that you can explain reality in a way that does not deny their own experience, and provides a pragmatic understanding of what needs to be explored and understood by all. In this role, a leader must carefully consider observable facts, potential consequences, and impacts. In many cases, leaders must think ahead of the curve, discern emerging trends, understand the perspectives of futurists, analyze data patterns, and extract insights that can forecast potential market opportunities. This can drive the development of innovative business products or solutions to address problems that may not yet be apparent to others. Sense-Making at its best is exemplified by innovative leaders who can articulate the past, the present influences, and the future implications of their discoveries.

You will need to develop your Sense-Making skill as a prerequisite for higher-level impact and influence in today's organizations. Factual data, analysis from multiple sources and ideas are proliferating exponentially. But the ability to process these pieces of information with calm, non-attachment, and mindfulness will greatly assist you in activating your creativity, innovation, and original ideas. Your brain must be in a relaxed state for new thoughts to emerge without blocking "out of the box" thinking, which might be exactly what you and your team need to advance. There's an old saying that says, "best ideas come to you in the shower." You must allow for the neurotransmitters to flow and do their work of making sense in your mind of what has been consciously and unconsciously absorbed. There is new research on learning that says that focusing on repeated attempts to learn one subject for hours is not as productive as varying subjects and moving from one topic to another in shorter periods of time. This promotes retention and activates different parts of your brain to learn faster and more creatively.

Sense-Making is also about learning and connecting insights through systems thinking so you can design your personal approach to receiving information, knowledge, and insights that you can connect to your current context and situation. Leaders at all stages of their maturity can benefit from it as it is a cumulative capability that will position you in a more consistent practice of reflecting, thinking about what's already in your power, and acting with professionalism and poise. This is also an opportunity for you to start validating your experiences, your history, your wins, and failures as well as all the lessons you have learned that may or may not be accessible to you, consciously. This is when meditation, quiet moments of breathing, and reflecting without judgment will help you recover experiences and events that will need to be reviewed through a different perspective as you connect dots and create new relationships between facts, observations, and insights. I often think about the difficulties I experienced as building blocks of my ability to cope with whatever comes at me. Developing this sense that you can get through whatever happens is an essential approach to Sense-Making for growth.

Exercise: In today's world there are plenty of challenging things for you to focus on and explore your Sense-Making skills. For this exercise, identify a subject that fascinates you, that intrigues you with its complexity. This could be a personal conflict in choosing the best way forward in your career, or it could be the overwhelming digital transformations across different industries. Now, for the twist: share your thoughts without letting your own biases get in the way. Originality is your secret weapon here. This might turn into a new business idea. Allow for weird thoughts, ideas and combinations of art, science and fun to come to mind. Consider exploring the Generative AI world with its challenges, opportunities, and tremendous potential to revolutionize how we work.

Bonus Exercise: Decision making in business. This exercise will help you gain awareness of your preferred ways to make decisions as well as assess what you will need to pay attention to when making decisions that impact others. Future-ready organizations expect all members of their workforce ecosystem to act with a leadership mindset, make sound judgments, express what needs to change, what capabilities to develop, and activate decision-making across the organization. Using your CARDS, focus on this important element of success in organizations today and tomorrow.

To develop decision making as a leadership skill, you will benefit from these questions:

1. Do I understand the root cause of the problem?

2. How ready are we to change and make these decisions?

3. What's the business case for a potential decision?

4. Why does it matter for the business, our customers, and our teams?

5. Who will ultimately make the final decision?

6. Who will be impacted by the decision?

7. What functions, business units, and teams should we seek advice from?

8. Who will be our partners in the execution of a potential project?

9. How are the external markets, partners, and networks dealing with this?

10. How will this decision create value for the business, customers, and people?

11. How much courage do you need if you don't have the empowerment to act?

If you want to practice, do this exercise with a colleague and brainstorm even better questions. After that, allow time to reflect on how you deal with changes, take responsibility for building the courage and confidence to make important decisions. Hint: Insecurities about potentially failing are universal, and your role is to do your best. Having all the data is not enough to help you decide. You will need to talk to a diverse network of people and allow for your curiosity to take you to the finish line. Remember to be honest and authentic and try not to procrastinate. Take the opportunity to think about employees and how to introduce change to a workforce that's distributed and diverse.

CHAPTER 12

Coaching & Transformation

Support the workforce on your journey to transform yourself and your organization.

Practice coaching.

This might be the most important practice for a career in leadership, whether you are leading yourself, others, or organizations. Coaching in its essence is a method of interaction you can use to help others tap into their potential and achieve success. It is a powerful catalyst of self-development when approached with an intention to learn about oneself and new ways of seeing and thinking about a situation. In the current evolution of the workplace, it's essential to integrate well-being into the fold of a holistic approach to coaching the whole person.

Coaching distinguishes itself from mentorship, sponsorship, advocacy, allyship, and counseling by placing the individual being coached in the driver's seat toward the achievement of their specific goals. As a coach, you're a skilled facilitator of reflection and self-discoveries, helping identify real obstacles and self-imposed limitations. Executive coaching and leadership coaching is all about willingness to search for new information, new perspectives, and ultimately allowing for new ways of learning and leading.

A leader is a coach with clear boundaries, objectivity, and empathy when helping others build their confidence. They do this by identifying their leadership blind spots, while strengthening their abilities and skills in preparation for new challenges. Coaching is a power skill, but it is also a disciplined methodology that requires education, practice, and for most, a certification. However, the necessary coaching skills are complex in nature and incredibly valuable for anyone interested in being a People Leader. And the first step is to understand that coaching methods, models, and frameworks vary depending on the type of coaching you choose to pursue. Providers may offer life coaching, career-coaching, leadership-coaching, executive-coaching, group-coaching, and a whole variety of specializations. Formal training might be offered by universities as full-programs, by organizations dedicated to this discipline, or by groups that have been formed around a type of coaching practice. And if you are a full-time employee in an organization, you will have the access to digital learning programs on coaching as a skill.

Time to learn by doing: This exercise will focus on your "coachability." But again, it is important to see coaching as a cluster of skills and accept that it's a profession that is deeper and more complex than you might think. For now, I will ask you to identify a professional challenge you are experiencing and find someone you know who has been coaching others. Focus on how open you are to being coached by asking yourself a few questions: Have I ever changed my mind because I was influenced by someone? Have I trusted others to help me figure out problems in the past? How do I react to authority figures? Once you have a coach, a course of six sessions would be a good start for you to get an idea of the process. Keep a journal with your authentic reactions, and all that comes up for you. This will help you shape the coach in you!

If you decide to coach someone instead of being coached for the exercise, please go ahead, and use the model below. This is a practical and simple approach I use in my short-term coaching engagements as a basic guide to best outcomes. In my experience, the coaching process is composed of four distinct phases. The IDEA Model defines the role of the coach in each stage of interaction with the "coachee" that fosters a dynamic flow of reflections, shifts, and options towards best outcomes. In this process, the coach will meet with the "coachee" for six sessions:

IDEA

A disruptive coaching model

❶ Identify Goals

❷ Disrupt Thinking

❸ Encourage Experimentation

❹ Activate Plans

IDEA: Identify, Disrupt, Encourage, Activate

Identify goals (Session I)

Building rapport and objectively identifying the goals for the coaching engagement are essential steps in shaping the scope of the work and focusing the conversation. It is imperative that you create a safe space for the sessions by establishing the rules for the engagement, including confidentiality, expectations, and openness to exploring options. You may enter this phase with statements and questions that help you define goals:

- We will have the opportunity to meet six times, and it would be helpful to start with your goals for our work together.
- What prompted you to seek coaching at this time?
- Have you identified what you would like to accomplish in these sessions?
- If I asked you to prioritize your goals for our work, what would you say is your top priority?

Disrupt thinking (Sessions II and III)

In this phase, the coach explores the current attitudes, perceptions, hopes and fears the coachee might be experiencing in order to assess their self-limiting beliefs, self-image distortions, and preconceived ideas and biases that may be interfering with their ability to see the problem with a fresh perspective. Using the third session to disrupt their thinking, the coach might ask probing questions to expand the coachee's view of themselves, including fears and aspirations:

- What kinds of actions have you taken so far to address these difficulties?
- What has been the result of these attempts?
- Have you shared these thoughts and experiences with any-one before coming to me? What have you learned from those interactions?
- You seem to believe you have exhausted your options. What makes you say that? What may be other ways to tackle this chal-lenge?
- What do you believe you would need to achieve these goals? What prevents you from doing what you think needs to be done?

- If I asked you to see this situation from the point of view of others involved, how would you reframe the situation and these challenges?
- You seem to believe you don't have what it takes to solve this, but if you did, how would you describe yourself having the skills, the courage, and the confidence to act differently?

Encourage experimentation (Sessions IV and V)

After assessing the coachee's current level of confidence, their hindering perceptions of themselves, and connecting more deeply with the subconscious behaviors, actions, and beliefs that may be interfering with their progress, you may provide your objective view of what you have observed in their statements about the situation and their own capabilities. Now it is time to encourage the formation of new neuropathways by focusing the coachee's exploration of a-ha moments, insights and empowerment:

- You have been clear about what you want to achieve, and in the last few sessions I noticed that you are allowing yourself to entertain new ways of viewing this situation. What have you learned about yourself that helped you open that door?
- We discussed the patterns of behaviors you tend to exhibit in these situations, and I heard you say you wish you had the courage or the skills to act differently. What if the option to do that was available to you?
- Coaching is about change and growth. In that sense, you are here to experiment with new ways of being, seeking, and doing. How about we begin to define what those changes will do for you and your career?
- You have been open about your true beliefs about yourself and these challenges, now allow yourself to go through the door

of possibilities. You made several discoveries about yourself, what could you put in place that would indicate that you are letting go of what's not serving you anymore? What can you start doing now that would make you proud?

- We have talked about potential shifts and new practices you may want to experiment with. What will you try that could give you the confidence you are moving toward your potential?

Activate plans (Session VI)

The last session of a short-term coaching engagement is always a mix of feelings, accomplishments, doubts, and all the emotions in between. By now, as a coach, you have been doing your best to avoid giving direct advice to your client. Hold your thoughts for a moment, and before starting the last session, think about how would you like this session to end? What do you expect your client to leave with? These are questions that will help you achieve a balance between perfection and progress. You might be inclined to criticize yourself for not being perfect. Accept it and move into your best self and offer your client your most authentic words that combine the work of your hands, your heart, and your head. You did the work, you helped your client explore their thinking, now it is time to offer what your heart is telling you to share. In my personal journey doing this work, I often navigate the integrity of the coaching approach and the intuitive nature of my leadership capabilities to find a way to share without crossing personal boundaries. This may help you as well. The line is drawn at that moment when you realize that you are placing the burden on your client to acknowledge you, to approve you, to support you, or to take care of you. That's when you know you've crossed the line.

Your goal in this session is to solidify shifts that may have occurred in your client's perception, reinforce the progress they have made, and most importantly, activate their potential to continue this journey of growing their abilities. Now your client will have the tools to identify self-limiting beliefs, acknowledge them as a passing thought, and move forward to explore their own potential by knowing that there is more to learn, more to share, and less to fear when you have purpose and clear goals. This last session is about activating their ability to coach themselves and allowing for fears to rise and still push forward with courage and confidence. Some statements you truly believe in and might want to include are:

- It's been inspiring to work with you and witness your willingness to explore your experiences with curiosity. Your willingness to be open to the discoveries you've made here are reflected in your growth.

- I would love to hear how you integrated this experience as a leader and what you believe will support your experimentation in forming new habits and new patterns of behavior in the future. What would help you maintain this growth disposition?

- I feel privileged to be part of this process with you and grateful you've allowed me to be on this journey with you. I felt your emotional commitment to this experience, and I know you will strive to reach your potential in everything you do. (I would only say this if I really felt the client gave it 100 percent of their effort in working with me.)

- You focused on specific goals with me, and I am sure there will be more opportunities for you to seek coaching in the future. Please know that the process of developing your leadership is iterative, non-linear, and most importantly, it is your choice to pursue it. Aim for progress, not perfection.

- You have been focusing on some actions you might take as a result of this process. How could you reinforce your courage and confidence as you activate your plans? Who is in your support system? What could you say to yourself when doubts emerge?

Leaders often seek coaching for an unspecified timeframe, and that's never a good arrangement since it leaves too much to be defined. I prefer to contract for three or six months. However, if you're a People Leader, you will need to master coaching others on the spot and sometimes you might have only one session with your direct report for a topic or situation identified by you or your team member. The most important thing to remember is to adopt the principles of coaching and stay out of the way of this intentional interaction by watching for your biases, opinions, and personal preferences.

The People Leader is a caring leader.

It's important to make sure your team knows they matter, both to you and to the organization. Show your commitment to their well-being by creating an environment where they can shine. Part of your job is keeping an eye out for signs that your team members are doing well. Leading people in today's workplace is more dynamic, and it means being extra aware of the role you play as a coach to your team.

So, what does coaching look like here? Well, it's a mix of positive conversations, giving props when they do great work, offering feedback, helping with career plans, and just being there for them as a whole person. As a People Leader, make sure you're giving everyone on your team equal time. Schedule regular one-on-one meetings and make it a safe space for them to chat with you about whatever's on their mind.

Coaching as a People Leader is flexible and agile in today's workplace. Sometimes you're helping with career stuff or performance feedback, and other times you're lending an ear and showing empathy for personal challenges. Coaching is a skill you'll use throughout your workday, and you'll get used to those spontaneous, unscheduled coaching moments that pop up from time to time. And don't discard the opportunity to coach yourself using similar questions. Coaching yourself to success is an individual strategy if you are open to new discoveries of the self in the social environment.

Navigate transformations.

Leading transformations has become the new normal, but it is still difficult for most employees to adapt to continuous changes in the workplace. Learning how to lead in a transformation has the potential to enhance your well-being and grow your value as a leader by applying an ambidextrous leadership style. All people, including contingent/fractional professionals and executive leaders won't be immune to the loss of control necessary for teams to progress during systemic changes. It's your ability to observe, listen, explore, and make sense of what's happening that will increase your capacity to assess your role in these transitions.

You are in control of how you understand and respond to transformative initiatives in the workplace, and even when you're not making decisions about what needs to change, you're an active member of the community of workers who will execute on these plans. Finding new ways to cope during a period of transition, you will be practicing your leadership skills and increasing your confidence in overcoming obstacles. There's no recipe for a perfect transformation and in fact, most of them fail to deliver due to many factors. First, leaders have the tendency to celebrate wins before the results, secondly, transformations are not fully accepted by all employees who will need to know how and why they must change, and thirdly, there are variables that can't be controlled such as an economic downturn, or a new player in the marketplace, or even lack of resources for the changes to be completed. In most of these efforts, leaders will make more cosmetic than systemic changes. You can't underestimate the mental, emotional, and physical efforts required for major transformations. Often, after a year or so, change fatigue sets in, and the energy to fully transform dissipates across the organization.

Despite the risks and potential setbacks, leading transformations is a critical experience that builds your capability to lead and fosters trust across the talent ecosystem. The skills you can use to adapt to ongoing changes in the workplace will continue to be highly valued and needed in business and organizational life, globally. You might have some of the skills necessary to cope with change, but it's also essential to develop the skills to lead in dynamic work environments through influencing and being able to articulate the value of the initiatives. From learning to adapt to championing changes, you will need to navigate the expectations others are placing on you as a leader, even if you are just working on a single workstream of the transformation. People are seeking certainty where there is none, they want to know what their company is transforming into, and as most humans, people need to know what, when, how, and why changes will be made. You must address them in a way that reassures the workforce with transparency and credibility. This will increase trust and confidence in the leadership of the organization, but these messages need to be managed well and consistently across the enterprise.

Leading a transformation is a skill that'll do you a world of good. Most organizations use it to boost efficiency, stay competitive, and meet market demands. Being on top of this game involves keeping an eye on market signals, knowing what's buzzing in your industry, and understanding your company's strategic goals. If you want to spot potential transformation opportunities, be proactive. Look for ways to simplify processes, find chances to pool resources, and let your creative ideas flow. Critical organizational capabilities are a big part of transformations, but not all business leaders are great at identifying, designing, developing, and deploying them. To get there, dig into customer data, scan the markets, analyze your competitors' skills, and check out the economic forecasts for your markets. All this groundwork will help you spot the capabilities that can supercharge your company's strategy.

Regardless of your role, understanding organizational capability will help you articulate value creation in a way that can be deconstructed to be shared in simple words. An organizational capability is something that a company has built to operate effectively. It consists of technology and platforms within an organizational design that allows for a workflow that optimizes resources, skills, and the people that deliver business outcomes. Financial reporting and analytics are crucial capabilities for organizations. They help uncover valuable insights that can benefit the business. Imagine a customer engagement system that makes everything super smooth—it's like a secret weapon that gives a big edge to a company. Now, here's the exciting part: spotting one of these game-changing capabilities can revolutionize a company. Think about a retail store that suddenly offers health care services in their shops. They'd disrupt multiple industries and gain a massive competitive edge. So, when companies decide to transform, you could be the person who suggests these game-changing capabilities. That's how you earn a stellar professional reputation and help your employer succeed big time.

There is no change without loss.

Continuous change and transformations can be emotionally tough because they often mean things won't stay the same, and that feels like a loss. But here's the deal: change always involves some kind of loss. It's like going through a breakup—there's a grieving process.

Think back to big changes you've faced. You might recognize these stages that have been established by psychiatrist Elisabeth Kübler-Ross in her work on the stages of grief and loss, and how most of us cope with them:

Denial: At first, you might pretend the change isn't happening. It's like when you're in denial about a breakup, hoping it's just a bad dream.

Bargaining: You start making deals with yourself, like, "If I do this, maybe things won't change." It's kind of like saying, "If I call them, maybe we'll get back together."

Anger: When big changes affect your job or life, you can get mad. You might blame leaders or the situation. It's like saying, "This is unfair, and I'm angry about it!"

Depression: It's normal to feel down when you realize the change is real. It's like when you finally accept the breakup is over, and you feel sad about it.

Acceptance: Eventually, you come to terms with what happened. You integrate it into your life and move on. It's like saying, "Okay, this is part of my story, and I'm ready to keep writing it."

These stages are a natural part of dealing with loss and change. Sometimes, it helps to talk to someone about it, like a friend, or a pro. But remember, acceptance is the final step, where you move forward with your story.

Becoming an organizational leader.

When you become an organizational leader, Organizational Effectiveness becomes a personal responsibility that demands consciousness and curiosity to achieve common goals. In fact, OE should be understood as the outcome of a leader's dedication to success. It takes focused intention to understand what roles team members are playing in any given initiative, as the work itself is shifting and becoming a fluid process of prioritization, with cross functional Objectives and Key Results (OKRs) as well as a blend of skills' clusters that build capability and value for the organization. You, as an individual contributor or as a People Leader, will need to adopt OE as a mindset to take personal accountability for process optimization, capability development, automation of tasks, and ineffective workflows. Performance Development is a key component of OE, which enables People Leaders to share coaching skills, knowledge of content for projects and topics, as well as guidance to ignite higher performance. Business performance is the outcome of Organizational Effectiveness reflected in the aggregate value the workforce produces that connects individuals and teams to the positive impact on the overall results of the organization.

We are moving away from performance management programs in which managers are processing the annual cycles of performance ratings, calibration meetings, and using outdated methods to force rank their people with percentages and other inefficient tasks to comply with systems of management that are not producing value. In the new workplace, OE must be sponsored by business leaders who are championing Performance Development, developing people's skills, including consciousness, curiosity, and courage to push their limits. Mihaly Csikszentmihalyi was a Hungarian-American psychologist who coined the term "flow" as a state of optimal performance in which humans are at their best when the challenge of their work meets their skills to the fullest. Flow suspends time and space in a mental state of focus and engaged energy. This might become your personal goal when working solo, and if you are a People Leader, finding a way to keep your team members in the state of mental focus will increase their engagement, their commitment, and engender learning in the flow of work as the norm.

On a personal level, performance development is something for you to practice, and use to enhance the quality of your work while achieving higher proficiency in relevant skills. That's why performance management will no longer be an HR responsibility in which processes are completed without major insights and extracted from the effort which is a very disliked process in today's workplace. Employees don't see why performance management cycles are so complex when they have no impact on the individual, or the organization. Yes, compensation will be impacted by some of the performance ratings in most companies, but the normal curve where 5 percent are Low Performers, and maybe 10 percent are High Performers, leaves little variation in 85 percent of your workforce. Is it worth the effort, the pushing, the nudging, and time required for completion of the process? Or should all employees be focusing on developing skills, progressing their careers, and creating value for customers and stakeholders? This is a perfect topic for a strategic conversation for senior leadership meetings to move the organization from process excellence to value creation.

Performance remains a critical component in Organizational Effectiveness, and you can start by assessing the elements that together are producing value for the organization, delivering the outcomes expected, and manifesting who you are as a High Performer. And here is where your consciousness will help you become aware of the personal impact you have on others as a contributor, collaborator, and catalyst. These elements of your performance are essential in building a positive reputation for yourself. I recall my first promotion at a global organization, and the moment was memorable not because I was surprised, but for what the executives said about me. One of them stated that I not only had the skills to do a great job, but the way I brought people together made it joyful to collaborate with me on projects. This was a defining moment in my career, and I will never forget that comment. That was a true moment of impact, and it encouraged me to seek roles of greater responsibility leading teams, strategic initiatives, and later, organizations.

As you probably know, people talk about others in the workplace and that's just how they relate to each other in their communities. That's why your reputation is part of the performance development plan you design for yourself, and for your teams if you are a People Leader. The plan needs to incorporate how you collaborate, how you show up, and how you build your Relational Credibility. Your ability to listen to others without judgment, without being attached to your own ideas, and focusing on making others successful, are hallmarks of a leader who uses their social power to elevate everyone around them. These are the leaders who build a following and have the greatest opportunity to lead successful missions. Being inclusive in your relationships and coaching others to raise awareness of themselves without shaming them, is going to build trust, and an emotional connection that leads to success. Sharing your knowledge, attention, time, energy, and experiences are key gestures for building a positive personal brand for yourself as a great collaborator and leader.

Organizational Effectiveness is a more complex concept that will challenge your ability to synthesize, integrate, and see the whole organization as an organic system in which all components come together to achieve business results. Organizational Effectiveness may be seen as the energy that fuels a high performing networked organization. OE incorporates decision-making, process optimization, organizational capabilities, organizational design, work design, new ways of working, leadership and power dynamics, diversity, inclusion, equity and belonging, as well as the cultural norms of an organization, inclusive of values, purpose and strategic priorities of the enterprise. In summary, OE is a complex power skill of a mature leader, and it demands courage, organizational mindset, and Adaptive Resilience from executives. There is no doubt your contributions to initiatives are directly and indirectly related to the skills and capabilities you bring to the teams you are working with.

Being a catalyst may be a differentiator of performance and has the potential to elevate your personal reputation to the level of a change champion. The catalyst role you play represents leadership at its best and must be highlighted as a behavior that inspires, energizes, and mobilizes others. When you are the catalyst of a team, you spark innovation and dialogue. Most often you will be unleashing the skills of others who were not coming forward with what they needed to do. Usually, being a catalyst is a behavioral signal that you have conviction in what you are communicating and embracing. All members of the new workforce will benefit from becoming catalysts for change, seeking to boost a high-performing culture, and team confidence. In this scenario, Organizational Effectiveness helps you see the elements of organizational performance that must come together to create the best workforce in your industry, with the best processes, culture, and strategies to win markets and new customers.

CHAPTER 13

Leading With Energy, Inspiration, and Impact

Human capabilities for the exponential era.

I am not bound to win, but I am bound to be true. I am not bound to succeed, but I am bound to live up to what light I have.
– Abraham Lincoln

The future of an organization can only be shaped by leaders who are perceiving signals, identifying market indicators, and sensing business opportunities by connecting external and internal forces of wisdom for the benefit of their followers. Moving from risk avoidance to proactive exploration of what's next, future-ready leaders know that advancements in technology are accelerating exponentially, and previously unimaginable possibilities are becoming part of a dynamic business strategy for the most innovative companies in the world. This is a shift in how leaders today are placing their bets, applying intuition when economists and futurists are not able to predict business trends with precision in a global fusion of unprecedented forces. There are too many variables to consider, and many disruptions are not yet visible to our current thought leaders and analysts. So, for you as a learning leader, the future is an exciting blank canvas, and you can invite the whole working community to color it with you as co-creators of this forward-looking strategy. Embracing leadership expressions of consciousness, curiosity, and courage, you can build inner strength and generate positive energy. This will help the collective leadership to spread across the workforce and the ecosystem of partners, customers, stakeholders, and shareholders. If you choose to take on the role of a visionary leader, you will inspire ambitious members of the workforce who are eager to offer you their discretionary effort toward a history-making movement. Visionary leaders instill excitement through shared purpose and play an essential role in cultivating high-performing inclusive cultures with distributed power and shared leadership. But it is up to you to expand your horizons and view your position with a fresh perspective.

In your career, moments of impact will become memories of transformative experiences. These special events might come in the form of advice that opens the doors to new ways of thinking, a co-creation with a team that elevates everyone's self-esteem with a collective accomplishment, or just a meaningful shared experience with people to whom you feel emotionally connected. These moments happen when you least expect it, and stay with you as a reminder that you were at your best when being authentic and present. The ineffable gift of transcendence through human connections can only happen when the moment aligns with your inner peace, blended with the inspiration of human kindness and loving relationships. Yes, love in the flow of work is something that exists, it revitalizes the soul, and motivates you to move ahead with confidence and optimism as you shape the future with others. Love is what shapes a community of like-minded people who are accountable for each other and care for their collective success.

There are no rules against exploring your emotional life to generate the energy that boosts leadership. You become a whole person when you allow yourself to feel joy within a group, building emotional intimacy with others, and reaching your self-actualization through beliefs and aspirations that include shared emotions with people in your life. In these special moments, the world suddenly slows down, and the Earth seems to stop, ushering goosebumps of transformation that trigger feelings of wonder without words or thoughts. Your ability to stay present for these experiences is what leadership energy is about. As you practice pure intention and reflect on what actions and behaviors create the conditions for positive impact, you enter a new level of leadership that's impossible to assess through tests or even evaluate in performance appraisals. If you can, go outside, be with nature, smile and reassure yourself that you are capable of more than you know, and breathe slowly and deeply until thoughts come and go, and peace is all that remains. This reflection is good practice to bring yourself to the present moment and reduce the recurring thoughts that hold you back. Be present without the mental narratives that distract you from your essential power.

When you advance to a business executive position, one of the greatest challenges you will encounter when leading the organization is the integration of many roles you must play in creating a holding environment for your people to thrive, explore, and expand their potential within a safe space. As a leader, your energy will influence what happens in meeting rooms. I heard a business leader say once, "Good leaders act as thermometers to sense the temperature in the room and adapt. Great leaders, however, act as thermostats." They set the temperature in the room through their presence, behaviors, and intuition. This concept of using intuition is worth a few words to ensure we are not mixing reactivity or gut feelings with this higher level of intuition. Intuition in this context is the power to synthesize your thoughts to allow the infusion of what you sense to be true, combined with your knowledge and experience in creating meaning before acting with decisive consciousness. Generating energy with clarity of purpose and being realistically optimistic are hallmarks of admired leaders who make balanced decisions and focus on executing strategic priorities.

Leadership in the second quarter of this century will be transcending technology and business operations to support sustainable performance and growth through the exploration of enduring human capabilities. In the environment where operational excellence can be achieved through automation of repetitive tasks, elimination of unnecessary work, and simplification of processes, leaders will prioritize outcomes and critical capabilities to remain competitive in their industries. Senior executives are already reaching the realization that Organizational Effectiveness is a value driver for the enterprise. These leaders also know that distributed power will drive business performance and that organizational design must be aligned to strategic priorities to avoid old habits of hierarchical architectures. Organizations will be designed for the activation of desired outcomes and promote collaboration without borders to reach best results while changing the way work is done within the new workforce ecosystem. Future-ready leaders like yourself will be leading from a higher state of awareness to build an environment that's inclusive, while dedicating time to knowing their customers, stakeholders, and members of the workforce to align everyone's mission with a value system driven by creativity, skills, and human-centered leadership.

You are pivotal in this current transformation in which companies, large and small, are struggling to find the best way forward for their businesses to thrive. The paradigms of our global economy are changing and the ripple effect in the system is disrupting usual thinking about productivity, talent engagement, leadership excellence and operating models that are rigid and inflexible. The concept of viability is forcing everyone to rethink how an organization can maintain fiscal integrity, mitigate risks, build strong relationships with suppliers, government officials, regulatory agencies, and global policy makers, while meeting the expectations of multiple communities connected to the company's strategy and goals. This is an exciting time for you as a leader to solidify your true north as you question your learned values, old professional boundaries, and integrate your ambitions, dreams, and financial needs. On this journey you will apply "CARDS" skills to experiences that challenge your assumptions and see new realities. In the process, you will engender timeless moments of impact that will help you share what you truly believe in with the next generation of leaders at all levels of the organization. Merging your abilities and the collective needs around you, will manifest a leadership style that activates work/life harmonization for the new workforce and build a high-performing ecosystem that's profitable and sustainable. The future of business will be grounded in leadership that elevates people above financial planning to unleash human skills as a competitive advantage in their industries.

Becoming an executive leader requires patience and focus. From individual contributor roles, you can begin the development of leadership skills that will greatly support your career and help you show the ability to act with Adaptive Resilience and a balanced judgment, grounded in data, insights, and as I said, your intuition. Demonstrating capacity for collaboration and sharing your expertise without sounding self-important you can manifest self-awareness, self-management, and engender psychological safety in support of an effort to build trust and deeper relationships. You will grow your skills at the pace you prefer, but it's incredibly important to develop your technical skills as well as your interpersonal dexterity with equal amounts of intention and enthusiasm. When you care about others, you will be an active listener, and these interconnected skills work to build a positive personal/professional brand and leadership profile. The complex skill of

Organizational Effectiveness will emerge organically when you have mastered the ability to gain insight, listen to feedback, and receive coaching in your career. Leaders who present themselves calmly and maturely have usually worked on their emotional lives as well. These leaders know how to stay present and reflect before jumping to conclusions. But remember, you don't need to be perfect to become a great leader.

I know it may sound like a Utopian version of business leadership, but the events of the first quarter of this century have shattered the notion of incremental improvements in operations, gradual shifts in the markets, and broken all the rules about where, how, and when work is done. The opportunity ahead of you is to redesign the work, reinvent the workplace, and embrace the new workforce composition that is weaving the fabric of culture, diversity, and inclusion in major organizations. Becoming a leader through the Personal Success Profile (PSP) is a process of integration in human development that accounts for the impact of our early experiences on our emotional development, as well as a life-long exploration of the psychological mechanisms we used to cope with life in our unique personality formation journey. Becoming a great leader is intrinsically connected to allowing yourself to become the person you want to be in every area of your life, without splitting yourself into personas for each role you play at home and at work. As I mentioned earlier, acknowledgment is not enough to change behavior, and adopting new ways of viewing the conflicts and dilemmas of life. Going deeper into an expression in consciousness with curiosity and courage can greatly enhance your ability to bring your best self to fruition. The road to a well-integrated life is not free of suffering, and at each stage of acceptance, you will be embracing your emotions with less fear, shame, and guilt. And when you achieve the state of self-acceptance, you will be able to replace negative and self-limiting beliefs with love for your whole self, kindness toward others, and compassion in all relationships that matter to you.

Leading an organization today demands dedication and devotion that will take as much time as you allow it to take. A few executive leaders in Fortune 500 companies have been able to manage their work in the flow of their personal lives, and this is something to consider as you plan your career and aspire to grow your responsibilities at work. Setting boundaries is an exercise in courage to prioritize aspects of your life that may not be independent from others, but strongly embedded in how you want to lead and maintain personal commitments to loved ones and your community. That said, organizational leaders must reach deep inside themselves to assess what could be an alternative to endless hours of preparation for a board meeting, or the insurmountable volumes of data. And here is where future-ready leaders can make a difference for the long-term sustainability of their organizations and their workforce. Applying common sense, with professional diligence in the discovery of facts, and listening to the sentiment of others, great leaders can establish themselves by accepting capacity limitations in their mental, emotional, and professional output.

If you are in a position of influence, your role has three major accountabilities. A senior leader must first address reputational risks and potential opportunities to grow brand visibility and value in the marketplace. This is accomplished by immersion in topics such as technology, cybersecurity, and external affairs impacting your industry. Second, it's also critical to keep an eye on outcomes-based performance to respond to revenue commitments and the execution of strategic imperatives that will satisfy board members, analysts, and your stakeholders. This topic requires a solid focus on operational cost management practices combined with the exploration of innovative offerings and products while maintaining margins and market share. And the third most important accountability has to do with your talent and the human capital. This is where you can have the greatest opportunity to lead the best teams in your industry and rewrite history by transforming your business and your workforce at the speed of quantum computing. This is Organizational Effectiveness at its best.

Talent development is a shared responsibility.

As a leader, when human capital is your competitive advantage, it makes sense to position talent development and the employee experience at the top of your priority list. The shifts in workforce demographics, work engagement models, demand for skills, and personal preferences emerging from the confluence of world events from the last ten years, are driving a new talent agenda in most organizations. From the traditional views of management to current disruptions in the workplace, there are new realities leadership teams must understand and leverage. The idea that talent is the concern of Human Resources is an outdated belief that has been debunked but not resolved. In a sense, talent development is everyone's business as much as leadership is everyone's responsibility in the new world of work. Models in role assignments, talent acquisition, organizational design, and the annual processes that we have grown used to in business are slowly losing value as they are not aligned to new ways of working. That said, we must organize a talent architecture that accounts for skills, technology adoption, creativity, collaboration, value creation, and attunement to the external network of customers, partners, and potential market opportunities available in the business ecosystem. This is as exciting as it is complex, which leads to the next point. Leaders of the future should strive to achieve balance between seeing the signals, and synthesizing the information necessary for better decisions. This is basically a state of calm and action. It becomes the manifestation of leadership virtues that inspire and support the well-being of the community we call the workplace.

Apply polarity management and quantum thinking.

There is a paradoxical dilemma inherent in business that needs to be managed by each leader in a way that satisfies multiple interest groups, but doesn't limit the multiple perspectives that need to be considered for a viable business strategy. The tension refers to the acceleration of technology and the expectations we place on leaders to be aware of everything that's impacting their businesses and respond to public concerns as well as behavioral economics. That's practically impossible when you have technology accelerating exponentially, and markets behaving erratically and unpredictably. These seemingly opposite realities must be managed to avoid binary thinking on the journey towards what I call "quantum thinking." In the new context, a leader won't be able to use their critical thinking in solving for these opposing forces unless they are able to stay present, exercise their Cognitive Mastery, and apply creativity. Simply said, to go faster, a leader must slow down and fully comprehend what the next steps need to be in order to manage dilemmas stemming from the speed of tech advancements, and the impact they have on the workplace, workforce, and work itself. Most often, reactive plans don't solve the conflicts and tensions in the organization as they stem from emotional reflexes and don't have the depth in strategic reasoning and clear awareness of the organization's tolerance for drastic changes in their operating models. Most senior leadership teams are allowing for group thinking to slow their decision making to a level of inertia that covers the root cause of the problem: lack of courage and discernment in challenging the status quo with a sustainable strategy for the business. And to do that, leaders must take risks and think differently about direction, connections, and the possibilities available when exercising "quantum thinking," where thoughts, ideas, and potential radical new ways of thinking might disrupt sequential ways of formulating strategic plans.

Quantum thinking refers to the possibility that valuable connections are not yet visible in the business ecosystem, and we must apply human capabilities to identify potential new ways of solving for the complexities of organizations of the future. A proactive approach to organizational disruptions will require executives to share power by activating leadership development in all members of the workforce with unwavering trust in each employee's ability to achieve greatness. The collective energy generated by a unified workforce is an unstoppable force of differentiation for an organization to win new markets and ignite innovation. As in quantum computing, we know that specific conditions in the environment must be met for those computers to function at their potential. The same principle can be applied to organizational leadership. The concept of power is inextricably connected to the idea of energy, which needs to be released to be utilized consciously and courageously by informal leaders of the organization. Innovation will emerge from divergent ideas and contributions from all dimensions of our diverse workforce community. To deny the opportunity for people to fully contribute with their best skills is hindering the progress of many industries fixated in protecting their history by disguising dysfunction with operational excellence, efficiencies, and core businesses that need to be respected for a delusional belief in maintaining an identity that no longer serves the organization. Intentionally exploring Organizational Effectiveness, leaders in shifting industries, will be moving with agility from products to services and other offerings as strategic actions that have the potential to save major organizations in the world from extinction.

Develop your role in shaping the culture.

Proactively shaping a new business culture through inclusive leadership and consciousness, you will be developing a sustainable, equitable, and resilient workforce that's equipped for the challenges of future disruptions. Maintaining a fluid open mind to partnerships, gaining new insights from external diverse networks, and allowing yourself to be the learner among your workforce, you will be modeling behaviors for the discovery of new opportunities with confidence. As a leader, your role is to identify conflicts, tensions across your businesses, and read the context of your industry and the organization's ecosystem, while ensuring everyone can contribute their ideas, apply their skills, and offer new perspectives on converging strategies. Prioritizing initiatives that are co-created with your people will boost their commitment to action and will ultimately make the energy of a team more positive. Your organization must be a talent magnet for ambitious informal leaders of all ages and backgrounds. The greatest leaders of the future will not be the ones coming up with the best ideas for the company, rather, they will be identified and admired for their listening skills and openness to individual contributors.

Leadership in the new context of a modern workplace is revealed through Sense-Making, radical collaboration and full engagement based on trust that builds psychological safety and respect for each unique individual. As a cultural practice, members of the workforce adopt these behaviors as a natural evolution to the humility demonstrated by leaders and the relationships based on deeper human connections. In the new workplace, every encounter becomes an opportunity to learn, and mastery is gained in the process of exchanging knowledge and sharing experiences. As the world changes at the speed of light, stars shine brighter when recognized for their uniqueness and purpose. Using all your senses and reinventing what it means to be a leader might be the only way forward when chaotic states of being are challenging us to overcome the passive power of silence. Knowledge will not be enough to respond to future challenges; conversations, debates, and open discussions will need to replace polite organizational exchanges. Experimentation and creativity will be the ingredients of competitive advantage in organizations that are ready for their quantum leap. Composing the workforce ecosystem of the future will demand curiosity about what's beyond the boundaries of your organizational walls. You might find treasures along the way if you take this journey with curiosity. Developing a new mindset of non-attachment to your ideas, values, and assumptions will allow you to explore trade-offs without fear, and see changes as natural stages of maturity your organization must go through to evolve and grow. Just like you and the people you lead.

In essence, organizations are organic, complex, adaptive, and dynamic systems activated by people who must be engaged in leadership development as soon as they enter the workforce. This will minimize the impact of natural tendencies to seek control and avoid changes as perceived threats. In addition, the workplace has been challenged by forcing functions that are inevitably transforming the way we think about where and how work gets done. The next big step in Organizational Effectiveness is the exploration of technology as complementary to human skills. This has major implications on how you as a leader must expand your understanding of organizational design, work design, and most importantly, organizational capabilities. The work is no longer a linear sequence of steps and activities that can be optimized by lean initiatives alone. The process of reinventing how value is created is changing the way teams are working together, silo organizations are sharing knowledge and resources, and how leaders are organizing skills and expertise around key value drivers instead of relying on formal roles. The deconstruction of work, the creation of new roles, and the opportunities for automation and simplification of work activities and processes are providing organizations with the greatest opportunity to increase efficiency while enhancing their effectiveness as a business. Leaders must start with the strategy of their organization, and translate it into critical organizational capabilities, and from there, begin the process of reinventing how technology and platforms can best deliver these capabilities, and design processes with a clear understanding of the skills and expertise required for the strategy to come to fruition. The discovery of these skills may lead to a less hierarchical, less siloed, and more collaborative organization based on the design and development of value drivers delivered to attain competitive advantage in saturated and overcrowded markets. To leap into the future through quantum thinking, a leader must allow for the flow of opportunities that were not considered even a few years ago. The ability to lead operating systems as opposed to static models will define the winners of the future. And as a leader you will be leading at the edge of the future with curiosity and courage to disrupt you own thinking.

The new employee experience is frictionless, fluid, and flexible.

I hope this book helps you attain an amazing career into a personalized journey of leadership skills—irrespective of your position, kind of work you do, and aspirations you have. It was written to inspire you to manifest your best self by reducing self-limiting beliefs and elevating your confidence. The leadership roles you decide to take on during your career will serve as key milestones in your development. The core principles of leadership are immutable. Leading by learning, sharing, and elevating others provides you with a best leadership blueprint for the new era of collective intelligence. Your ongoing challenge is to remain centered during storms and disruptions, as these often trigger emotional reactions which may destabilize your coping skills. A state of calm and conscious awareness will have a positive impact on your well-being. Reflect on how to best support others while staying connected to yourself, your consciousness, and the universal power that permeates every moment of our lives as leaders who channel the transcendent energy of our collective experience.

RESOURCES

Csikszentmihalyi, Mihaly. *Flow: The Psychology of Optimal Experience* (New York: Harper & Row, 1990), 82

Dweck, Carol. *Mindset: The New Psychology of Success* (New York: Ballantine Books, 2006), 52.

Gardner, Howard. *Five Minds for the Future* (Boston: Harvard Business Review Press, 2006), 26.

Heen, Sheila and Douglas Stone. *Thanks for the Feedback: The Science and Art of Receiving Feedback Well* (New York: Penguin Books, 2014), 81.

IBM Institute for Business Value: CEO Study (IBV, 2010)

Kübler-Ross, Elisabeth. *On Death and Dying* (New York: Macmillan, 1969), 45.

Wadhwa, Hitendra. *Inner Wisdom, Outward Success: 7 Mindful Steps for Overachievers.* Currency, 2023.

Winsor, John. *Open Talent: Where Competency Meets Desire and Knowledge Meets Networks.* Sausalito, CA: Netformic Publishing, 2020.

ABOUT THE AUTHOR

Wagner Denuzzo is a transformational Latino executive leader with a breadth of experience in Leadership Development and all aspects of the future of work.

He specializes in developing leaders at all levels of the organization, emphasizing managerial capabilities to drive performance, while caring for the well-being of employees. He has a proven ability to support diverse leadership teams through continuous changes. Wagner is an inspiring speaker, helping leaders build resilience and adaptability.

Prior to returning to his own business as a consultant, speaker and author, Wagner held successful positions in Fortune 500 companies.

He was the VP and Global head of Leadership and Management Development at IBM during the tenure of the first female CEO, where he created an award-winning digital Leadership Academy, which became the second most visited platform at IBM.

Wagner began his career as a psychotherapist and employee assistance counselor, and expanded his expertise into executive coaching, training, consulting and HR strategy. He now contributes to several publications on the future of HR and Leadership, and advises HR StartUps on their go-to market strategy.

He lives in Westchester, New York.